blagging it

James Moore is a freelance national newspaper journalist and, among others, has written for the *Sun*, the *Daily Mirror*, the *Daily Express* and the *Sunday Telegraph*. His blagging credentials include smuggling fake drugs into a maximum-security prison to expose weak security, talking his way into a private party for former MI5 boss Stella Rimington, and attempting to ice-skate with Olympic Gold medallists Torvill and Dean.

Copywriter Paul Nero worked for newspapers, TV and radio, before starting his own company in 2001. After attending a small, unknown college, where he excelled as an acrobat, he blagged his way into a succession of jobs to get his hands on freebies such as hot-air balloon flights, a trip to the Olympic Games and an attractive pair of stilts. He retired to Cornwall at a ridiculously young age and is now learning to box.

blagging it

How to get almost everything on the cheap

PAUL NERO
AND
JAMES MOORE

Michael O'Mara Books Limited

First published in Great Britain in 2004 by
Michael O'Mara Books Limited
9 Lion Yard, Tremadoc Road
London SW4 7NQ

A CIP catalogue record for this book is available from the British Library

ISBN 1-84317-104-X

3 5 7 9 10 8 6 4 2

Designed and typeset by Envy Design

Printed and bound in Great Britain by Cox & Wyman Ltd, Reading, Berkshire

contents

introduction

As everybody knows, the best things in life are far from free: designer clothes, fast cars, holidays abroad – even sex has a financial and emotional price tag. But if you want to wallow in riches or be treated like royalty there is an answer. You need to blag it. This is the book that tells you how.

Blagging It is packed with great ideas that work. Here are the tools you need to stop shelling out and start wising up, with proven ways to get more out of life by putting in less. Discover how to wheedle your way to success in the workplace, shave the price of a meal out and exploit gullible people to your advantage. Learn too from some real-life blaggers.

Happily, you don't need to break the law to blag your way through life. Blagging isn't about committing theft or fraud – it's about getting your own back on the system. So be brazen. Be bold. Be proud to be a blagger.

Of course, when you blag, the aim is to have a bit of fun and see what you can get away with, but if in doubt, apply a simple test. Consider whether your plea, 'I read it in a book called *Blagging It*,' will impress the judge very much.

Finally, if you have a new blag to share or know the perfect place to get something for nothing, tell us at the *Blagging It* website at *www.blaggingit.com*.

Happy blagging.

publisher's disclaimer

The publisher wishes to make clear that this is a work of humour and the advice and opinions represented in this book are not intended to be taken seriously in any way. Neither the authors nor the publisher shall be liable or responsible for any loss or damage arising from any information or suggestions in this book.

blagging it...
shopping and money

How to blag a discount

Blaggers should never pay full price for anything if they can help it. Shop till they drop (the price) with these tips.

Presents – and the cash too

Take back not just the presents you don't like, but the ones you do as well. Get your money back, then buy them again at the January sale price. Think of it like a double gift from your friends and family: you get the present and some cash.

Many shops allow a period of grace around Christmas for people to return unwanted presents for a refund, providing you have a receipt (they may just exchange the goods, or give you a credit note if not). They don't have to do this, they're just being nice. That doesn't mean you can't take advantage.

There's a mark on this, look!

There is *always* something wrong with whatever you're buying. A small scratch on a toaster, a slight scuff on a new shoe; something you can see, but the staff or manager probably can't in this light. They are just a tiny way from a sale – and without a sale, there's no profit. Better that they sell to you now, rather than have something stuck on their shelves indefinitely.

Try it with perishables too. If some food is very close to its expiry date, cut a deal, particularly if it's late in the day. You can even do this on long-distance trains. The nearer the buffet car gets to its destination, the less likely it is that all the grub will be sold. Name your price for the sandwiches and see what happens. Leave this too late though and they may have been sold to some other blagger and you'll go hungry.

Speak to the organ-grinder

Department heads have more leeway to cut a deal than you may think, so you may have to bypass the assistant and ask for their boss. Take care though to pitch your request to see the right level of manager. It's often better to ask to speak with the department head and not the overall manager, who is likely to be busier and will resent you pulling him or her away from other tasks.

You've just moved house

Bizarre as it may seem – particularly if you haven't moved home for a few years – many stores will give you discounts just because of the upheaval you're going through. They think that if you have just moved, you're going to need to spend a lot of money doing your new place up. DIY stores offer loyalty cards for home-movers. Just tell them your new address, and you can get a 10 per cent discount for up to a year at Focus, for example. Some of the larger stores don't even ask you to prove it. Just load up a crate of stuff and, when you're at the till, tell them you've had to stock up for your move.

Show your pension book ...

... and if you don't have one, take a pensioner who does. Many shops give discounts to senior citizens, so it's worth taking along ageing relatives when you shop at DIY stores and garden centres. Some pubs and restaurants offer cheaper meals to pensioners, so it's worth getting Granny to order. As elderly people don't eat much, you get the meal, she gets the scraps.

At the opposite end of the age range, students get discounts at bookshops, cinemas, hairdressers and gigs. Sign up for an evening class and you could be eligible for an NUS card. No need to go to lectures.

Join the club

If you've got a responsible job, do your shopping at warehouse club stores. You need to be a member, but they are often not too fussy about who they take (which is just as well). Check out CostCo, for example – a trade cash-and-carry store that is decidedly no-frills. Lots of the products are on pallets, waiting for you to pick them up. Among the members of the public they are happy to serve are police officers, dentists, members of the armed forces and people who work in banks. Be warned – as they cater mainly for businesses, VAT is added at the checkout and isn't included on each price ticket. So if an item costs £4.99 and you're down to your last fiver, you can't afford it.

Use multiple complaints

Check receipts, particularly at supermarkets that offer discounts when you buy multiple packs: buy one, get one free, that kind of thing. It doesn't always ring through correctly at the checkout. Don't say anything at the time, but once you get home, write letters of complaint both to the local store and the head office. You may find you get two replacements or two sets of vouchers.

Stick it on a store card

Store cards provide just about the most expensive way to borrow, this side of a loan shark. Yet, surprisingly, the rich are most likely to carry them. However, they use them wisely and rarely pay interest.

So, get as many store cards as you can. (The fact that it costs the shops money to recruit you is good enough reason on its own – but always pay them off right away, so you don't pay interest.) Then only use them when there's a special discount day.

You often get 10 or 20 per cent off for the first week – so take all your friends and pay for their purchases too. Charge your friends the full amount – it's no loss to them – or, if you're feeling particularly generous (unlikely), split the difference.

Women buy best

Statistically, women are better at finding bargains than men so, if you're a man, it makes sense to your pocket, if not your stress levels, to take along a girlfriend when you head for the shops.

On the downside, women also spend almost twice as long on their shopping trips, averaging two hours to a man's seventy-two minutes, which almost doubles the amount of time to find the bargains and to buy plenty more stuff.

When shopping with a partner, women should encourage their men to buy them something at around the seventy-two-minute mark. Wanting to get away by this time, he is more likely to dip his hand in his pocket.

When returning home with an armful of carrier bags men are more likely to say: 'Look how much I've spent', while women say: 'Look how much I've saved.'

How to blag it at the supermarket

Counter the deli queue

Deli counters often have a ticket-based queuing system, and this can mean a long wait at busy times. But there is a way to jump ahead. Collect as many of these used tickets as you can by never handing them in when it's your turn and snaffling a few extra each time. When you arrive at the deli counter in future, you'll always have the appropriate ticket.

If someone else claims the number when it's called, blame the machine and allow them to go first. You'll still jump the queue and look scrupulously polite into the bargain. Some of these tickets do have the date on them, but it's usually so small that no one notices or asks for it.

Become a 'freegan'

Just because food is past its sell-by date doesn't mean it isn't still perfectly good to eat, yet stores are still compelled to throw it out. So go to the bins behind supermarkets and get your groceries for free. It's a pastime that has become so popular – even among people who can afford to do their shopping inside the store – that it has acquired its own name: freeganism.

Wear headphones

Supermarket muzak is designed to lull you into a false sense of shopping security. On quiet Monday mornings, its leisurely, relaxed chill-out sounds encourage customers to take their time, stay longer in the aisles and spend more money. On busy Friday evenings, they play music to race round by because they want to get more people through the tills at breakneck speed, buying things they don't really need. Avoid the psychological games and listen to your own tape (of chants that say 'look for bargains, look for bargains').

Phil Calcott: feeling fruity

Sharp-eyed supermarket shopper Phil Calcott thought a Tesco loyalty-point scheme was bananas, but he couldn't resist taking part. For every 3 lb of bananas shoppers bought for £1.17, Tesco gave £1.25 on their loyalty card. Needing no more excuse to take every banana in the store, Phil shelled out £367 for half a ton of them – and got £392 back. With £25 and almost 942 lb of bananas profit, Phil was delirious with fruity happiness: 'I realised I was making 8p a time and could not lose. It was great fun,' he said.

How to haggle in a chain store

Never pay for delivery

Buying something bulky that needs delivering? Cheeky stores will try to add £15 or more to the advertised price, just for the privilege of selling it to you. Just as you're handing over your credit card, tell them that you never pay for delivery. If they fuss, start walking away: most shops won't want to lose a sale for something so trivial, especially when their delivery van will be on the road anyway.

If you pay cash, your hand is stronger still, particularly if you only take along the amount you need to buy the product – and perhaps a bit less so you can negotiate a discount.

Beat the price promise

Just because a shop says it has the cheapest prices, doesn't mean it's true. Neither should it stop you haggling for an even better deal. When you see that a store promises to beat another shop's price – and perhaps even give you a bit more too – make up a quote. They may want to check, but often they don't, especially if your suggested price isn't too outrageously different. Drop the name of the manager of a competing shop – they all wear name badges – to add credibility. This is the retail equivalent of playing one parent off against another.

Haggling is the law

Don't be fooled by price tickets – the price isn't fixed at all. Price tags represent the store's offer to you. Look upon them as the ceiling price that you can be expected to pay; the store's opening gambit. They don't have to charge you the advertised price and you are not compelled to pay it. Don't be concerned just because you're in a department or chain store and not a market. The same laws apply to all retailers.

I want more

When prices have been reduced already, it's a sure sign there's more room for negotiation. The shop is clearing space for new lines, so press for an even greater reduction – you're helping them out, after all. In furniture stores, pieces from the previous season that are meant to be part of a set may be left over with nothing that matches. You can get 90 per cent or more off original prices.

Interest-free interests you ...

... but only because you know it costs the shop money to arrange finance for you. Tell the salesperson you're happy not to take advantage of the interest-free deal, as long as you get a discount. As a general rule, it costs them about 5 per cent of the purchase price, so you should get that sum in your pocket. If you can pay cash, rather than by credit card, it could knock a further 3 per cent off. Call it a round 10 per cent and the deal's done.

REAL-LIFE BLAGGER

Kathleen Robertson: suite revenge

Avoid the hazards of badly behaved children in the shops – unless you can make a mint from them. When Kathleen Robertson tripped over a nightmare child and broke her ankle, she sued the furniture store she was browsing in – and won. Victory was all the sweeter because the bawling brat was her own small son. She hobbled away from court in Texas $780,000 the richer.

How to blag it with expensive goods

Hot stuff from the office

Last year's cutting-edge computer is today's dinosaur and companies need to upgrade their kit constantly to stay ahead. If they're nice, they give their old equipment to schools and charities. If they aren't nice, they try to flog it. Do them a favour – offer to buy it. It will save them the hassle of having it collected and all that paperwork. Some of them will say it's a health and safety risk to let private individuals remove stuff, but take the risk – unless you really think your boss is out to electrocute you. And if you do get zapped you (or your next of kin, if you're dead) can sue.

The pen that lasts a lifetime

Try to buy products with lifetime guarantees. A stylish pen might cost you more than £100, but over the course of a lifetime, it's a classy bargain.

If it breaks because of a manufacturer's fault, they'll fix it. If the damage is accidental, they won't – but your home insurance should cover you for accidental damage. You never have to buy a posh pen again.

Get a designer bathroom at bog-standard prices

Want a designer kitchen or bathroom, but don't want to pay designer prices? Ring a fancy firm that offers free quotations. They'll send a designer round to draft your plans – before you decide you don't want to go ahead. Use their great ideas, of course, but get the work done by someone cheaper.

Furniture madness

Showroom sofas get scruffy, with all those people flopping on them all day. Demand a hefty discount – stores tend to cut the prices of showroom models eventually anyway and you're making a 'bird-in-the-hand' offer now. Even if you pay to have the thing re-covered, you make a substantial saving.

How to be showered with gifts

It's better to receive than to give, as the saying goes. So increase the chances of being given the perfect present.

Say you're leaving – then stay
Announce your plans to leave your job, but don't actually resign. Hold a farewell drinks do – then say you couldn't possibly leave all these nice people in light of all their wonderful tributes – but thank you for the presents.

You're ill
A call round your friends to say you can't see them this weekend because you're bedridden should have them coming to you with books, fruit and muffins. Emphasise you're not contagious – but you've been unable to get out to do your own shopping and you're running out of food.

The present-price index
Before handing over presents, replace the genuine price tag with another – artfully torn to look as if you've tried to remove it – of much greater value. Your friends will feel they at least have to match this amount when they buy something for you. For every pound you spend, aim to get a fiver back.

How to blag cheap chic

Dead men's clothing
Buy your clothes from charity shops in posh areas. Look for garments with stylish timelessness. Then, even if they've been worn by local dead people, you'll appear suave.

You'll even look much richer when you buy good-quality clothes cheaply than you would getting down-market (but more expensive) clobber on the High Street. And when you look wealthy, you get many of the benefits of being wealthy, like attractive hangers-on.

It doesn't fit after all

An important occasion, like a job interview or a night out, deserves a snazzy outfit. So choose exactly what you want, even if it's outside your price range, take care when you wear it, then take it back the following morning and ask for your money back. Legally, you're not entitled to a refund, but some stores have a policy of accepting returns within a certain number of days, provided you have your receipt – and provided you haven't worn it (hence the reason for care). Do leave the price tag on, but don't let it show when you're out.

Grill a personal shopper

Many big department stores offer a free 'personal shopping' service – someone who helps you pick clothes that suit you down to the ground, in the expectation that you will spend an absolute fortune. Milk them for their style advice, then leave without buying anything and nip somewhere cheaper to get similar styles at a fraction of the price.

Make me over

Just before you set off to a party, ask for a free makeover at the cosmetics counter of a department store. Many will be happy to oblige – again, in the hope of a sale. You walk out looking fabulous – without having to buy any of the products. This isn't just limited to women. Men should pitch up at stores like Selfridges or Harvey Nichols and ask for advice about their blemishes.

Goodies are free when you know where to look

Why pay – when so many people want to give you things for free?

Music to your ears

Some record stores allow you a grace period in which you can take a CD back for a full refund if you don't like it. It's great customer service (how many times have you bought a dud album on the basis of one good track, only to regret it?), but plays into the hands of seasoned blaggers.

As most people listen to CDs frequently in the first few weeks, before shifting them to the back of the shelf to make way for even newer buys, it makes sense to use record shops like a lending library. You must not make a copy of the CD, of course, but listening and returning is fine – and part of many stores' policy.

Have a good whine

Wine shops play the same customer-relations card as music stores. If you don't like the wine, even if it's perfectly good, just say so, and many shops will give you your next purchase free. Some may require you to bring back the dregs that you haven't managed to down before deciding you didn't like it after all. They probably won't fuss if you drink three-quarters of the bottle before putting the cork back in.

Read them your rights

Bookstores don't mind if you read virtually the whole book before buying (or replacing) it; in fact, they actively encourage it. Many provide comfortable armchairs and sofas, and some of the larger chains have even installed coffee shops for you to sit down in with your book. It's a library by any other name.

Get fruity

Fruit is one of the most common freebies you can find (along with boiled sweets). Check out hotel reception areas and the front desk of health clubs. You may not be a member of the club, or staying at the hotel, but lobbies are busy places. You'll rarely be stopped when you help yourself.

They've put fruit out as a way to brighten the environment and make customers happier. They should be pleased you like their initiatives.

Buy a share and let a company treat you every year

As a company shareholder, you're entitled to attend the annual general meeting. One share will get you on the register. Choose companies with a reputation for fantastic hospitality at their annual bashes.

Many put on a fine lunch, with wine and beer, and often they give freebies – books, records, videos are all available when you select the right firm. It will cost you a few pounds to buy your share, but as you get a day out every year, think of it as a timeshare.

Electronic gadgets

Cut costs on buying batteries for your remote controls by popping round to your friends' houses and substituting your old set for the ones in their device. Keep them in the dark about your wicked deeds by swapping over your dud lightbulbs too, but do it in daylight to (a) prevent it being discovered until they turn the lights on that evening, and (b) avoid burning your fingers.

REAL-LIFE BLAGGER

Hetty Green: skilful skinflint

Witch of Wall Street Hetty Green was one of the richest Americans who ever lived, and was even more famous for the stingy way in which she garnered her fortune. As a child in the nineteenth century, Hetty wouldn't light the candles on her birthday cake so that she could return them the next day for a refund. She only paid for the dirty parts of her garments to be washed – a sleeve here, a cuff there – and warmed food on radiators, rather than turn on a costly stove.

How to blag your way to the front of a queue

Queue first

We've all encountered those irritating people who get to the checkout and then say, 'Can you just keep an eye on my basket for me?' while they go off and get more stuff. Heed their skills. Throw a couple of items in a basket when you go to a supermarket, then start queuing. Get someone to look after your place, and then go off and do your real shop.

Smile

When you're good-natured, people will do unexpectedly nice things. Be courteous in the line, then you can make up every story under the sun to blag your way to the front. Would you turn down someone who has raised his hat and bidden you a cheery 'Good morning' when he asks a moment or two later if he can go before you because he can hear his dog whining outside?

The correct response to anyone asking to shove in front of you because they only have a couple of items is to ask why they've come into a large supermarket just to get one or two things. Keeping them in their place (behind you) is an honourable public service and helps put a stop to selfish behaviour.

Get angry

Whingeing about the service you have received will increase the chances of a manager appearing and dealing with you. Quickly calm down and ask him if you can pay him for the goods you want. You should be served more quickly so they can be rid of you.

Clear the queue

Go to shops on busy roads with no car park. Loudly say that you've seen parking attendants wandering around outside, slapping tickets on vehicles like there's no tomorrow. You should find the queue disappears in seconds.

Create a distraction

Get a mate to pretend to collapse near the queue and then jump in as everyone else rushes to help.

Have the right money

Nip past someone saying that you have the right money and leave it on the counter. You can't be arrested if you have actually paid for something, and besides, you're only trying to help speed things up for everyone (although you may be delayed when the alarms go off because the security tag hasn't been cancelled).

REAL-LIFE BLAGGER

John Fashanu: beggaring belief

Former England soccer star Fashanu blagged his dream home by paying a tramp £300 to stand in a queue. When he found out that he was competing against other buyers in the race to land a London flat, and would have to queue outside the sales office to be sure of success, he paid someone else to do the legwork.

How to blag it when shopping on the Internet

How are you spelling that?

You may know how to spell, but some people don't. Others simply can't type and make mistakes entering their goodies when they sell them on auction sites like eBay. As misspelt products don't turn up in text searches, they don't attract many bids. One buyer snapped up three Compaq laptop computers for next to nothing simply by asking for 'Compacts' instead.

Get a robot onto it

An Internet shopping robot will track down the cheapest prices and even take delivery charges into consideration. The robot – or 'shopbot' if you want to be geeky about it – is nothing more than a website that searches lots of other websites to find the product you want at the best price. Try *www.kelkoo.co.uk* or *www.pricerunner.co.uk*. Shopbots are best used for commodity goods that can easily be stored in warehouses and delivered cheaply – like books, CDs and DVDs.

Go the long way round

Instead of going to retail sites directly, take a trip first to sites that have partnerships with the places you want to shop at and that give you a discount for doing so. To encourage you to keep shopping through them, these discount sites often give you cashback into the bargain and award points for completing surveys. For nothing more than a bit of additional time spent surfing, you save money when you spend with big-name stores and get a bit of extra cash too. Try intermediaries like *www.rpoints.com* or *www.greasypalm.com*.

How to make money out of credit-card companies

Tool up your imaginary friend

Look out for deals when you sign up a second cardholder. It could be a free gift, it could be cash. No need for the second cardholder to be alive, let alone married to or living with you. Just name a name and they'll send you a card for your imaginary friend so they can hit the shops. This friend doesn't need to sign anything, because the card is linked to your account. That means you're liable if they run up a large bill. As they don't exist, that's unlikely. Chop up the card when it arrives.

Zero sum games

Catch out credit-card companies. Bank their money.

Look for cards that lend you money at 0% interest by paying cash into your bank account (they sometimes issue cheques that you can write to yourself). Borrow a large sum and stick it straight into a high-interest savings account.

If you put £5,000 on a credit card and you don't pay interest, the cost to you is zero.

With that same £5,000 in a savings account paying, say, 4%, you make £200 a year. Many 0%-interest deals last six or nine months – so you get

£100 or £150 profit – just for signing the forms. All you have to do is pay the money back on time – and that's easy because it's in your savings account. Alternatively, transfer the balance to another card with a 0% offer. Don't be tempted to spend the money you've borrowed – and do remember to pay back the minimum amount each month. Sometimes they catch you out by insisting you have to spend a small amount each month.

Offers like this drop on to the doormat every day of the week. Run five of these blags in a year and you might earn around £750. But do check the terms and conditions.

How to cut your phone bill

The one-ring phone call
So you want to chat to a friend or relative on the phone. Make sure you don't pay for the call – let it ring once and then ring off. Because your mobile will display their number, and on landlines they can check with 1471, they'll think you got cut off and they will call you. Few people are cheeky enough to ask you to call them back. If they complain, say your phone doesn't seem to be making outgoing calls properly.

Take care with voicemail
It may be polite to record a personalised greeting on your answerphone or voicemail, but it's certainly not profitable. Callers are less likely to leave a message if they get through to one of those awful electronic messages that say, 'Your call cannot be taken at the moment.' You might think no one ever calls, but then you never have to call them back.

'I'm in a tunnel ...'
To shorten calls, pretend your hearing is going or that reception is cracking up (even on a landline). Buy a sound-effects device that attaches to your phone and plays realistic building-site noises, and shout: 'I can't hear you.' It's the perfect excuse to hang up.

Alternatively, make a rapid 'pip-pip-pip' noise and say you haven't any more change.

Juggle handsets
If you must call someone else's mobile (always an expensive mistake), do it from your own mobile, not your landline. It's almost always much cheaper.

REAL-LIFE BLAGGER

J. Paul Getty: ringing up a profit

Oil baron Getty was so careful with cash that he installed a pay-phone in his mansion to stop guests making calls for free. When asked for the reason, the mean-spirited millionaire said it saved visitors the embarrassment of having to settle their phone bills at the end of their stay.

How to blag your way out of debt

Go bankrupt
For some people, it's the ultimate embarrassment and something to be avoided at all costs, but you can do it legally and escape from the people who are after you for money. Personal bankruptcies are on the increase. Even students are getting in on the act: borrowing wildly to fund top-up fees and living expenses and then wiping out the debt right after graduating.

Beware. You might not be able to get any credit until you're later discharged from bankruptcy.

Sell up
Someone, somewhere is willing to buy absolutely everything you own. Check the newspaper classifieds, advertise on eBay, think creatively. Sell your footwear to a shoe fetishist, flog tap water as bottled water, rent your room on a time-share basis when you're out at work.

Get others to support your extravagant lifestyle
No need to be ashamed. If you spend more than you earn, ask others to make up the difference. The advent of the wired world has demolished

the barriers to begging. You can now go cap in hand across frontiers and ask kind-hearted strangers to help buy the consumer items of your dreams. A US web-beggar asked for thousands of dollars simply to buy a new lorry – and visitors to his website made huge financial pledges to keep him trucking.

REAL-LIFE BLAGGER

Karyn Bosnak: beg spender

Karyn, a self-confessed shopaholic, indulged herself in expensive designer clothes, $387 haircuts and a $394 facial – then set up a website to ask strangers to pay off her $20,000 debt. She said: 'Please help me pay my debt. I didn't hurt anyone by spending too much money. I was actually helping out the economy.' Amazingly, visitors to her site gave her the cash she needed. Now the cheeky ex-TV executive has even written a book about her stunt called *Save Karyn*.

How to delay paying bills

Your cheque is in the post
Never pay by debit card – and only use credit cards for items that cost more than £100 (where you get added legal protection). With a debit card your money goes more-or-less instantly. Paying by cheque causes companies more hassle and costs them money – so they might want to give you a discount instead. Not only do they have to remember to pay your cheques in, as they take time to clear you have use of your money for longer.

Post-date your cheques, forget to sign them or get the name of the recipient slightly wrong, for a delay that's easily explainable as a mistake. Mailing a new cheque will take days.

'Invoice me'
Whether it's a friend to whom you owe money or a tradesperson who has done work for you, ask for a printed invoice. Tell them it's to make sure your accounts are up to date for the taxman.

Wait for a red-letter day

Wait until the bill turns red before you cough up. Big business in the UK holds up £20 billion in outstanding payments, so why shouldn't you do the same?

REAL-LIFE BLAGGER

Gary Cooper: dollar signer

The Hollywood actor, famed for his tough guy roles, favoured paying by cheque. He knew that rather than cash it in, starstruck recipients preferred to frame and display his payment, to prove they had met the celebrity.

blagging it ...
when you travel

How to blag an upgrade on an aeroplane

Taking that valuable left turn into business or first class when you board a plane is costly: often ten times the price of an economy seat on transatlantic trips. Rich people don't turn right on planes, so you need to blag it.

Look the part

In the parlance of airline stewards you have to be 'SFU': *suitable for upgrade*. You're more likely to achieve this prestigious classification if you:

- Wear a suit or very smart casual clothing (designer casual labels).
- Don a dog collar (clergymen are favoured).
- Wear shoes, not trainers.
- Carry quality luggage.
- Use a platinum or gold credit or charge card.
- Wear discreet quality jewellery: a stylish watch says a lot.
- Sign your documents with an expensive pen.

Airlines upgrade people when the flight is full, not empty. By moving those they've classed as SFU up a cabin, they release economy seats for paying passengers. Irritatingly, a flight can be a third full, with plenty of spare business-class seats going begging, and you won't be offered an upgrade.

They only do it when the pressure is on. So travel at peak times for this perk; at other times, you're more likely only to get the flight you paid for.

Make an enquiry at check-in
A polite request can only be refused. If you don't ask, you're less likely to get. But avoid the tacky 'Any chance of an upgrade?' line – check-in clerks hear this dozens of times a day. Build a relationship in the limited time you have. Perhaps you have worries about deep-vein thrombosis. It could be a useful time to mention it (subtly, of course – so you shouldn't use DVT's common airline name: Economy Class Syndrome, but the connection should be obvious nonetheless).

Register with every frequent-flyer programme going
Members of frequent-flyer clubs are more likely to be offered upgrades – and kept informed of special deals. You can always use the points to upgrade when your polite request has been declined. Even a card at the most basic level makes you more important than the vast bulk of travellers. You won't get anything most of the time, but when the flight is almost full, your card is positively marked.

You're a VIP
Make an official-looking stamp that says 'VIP customer – upgrade where possible' and slip it in the envelope that your tickets come in (don't deface the tickets themselves, as this could cause problems).

Remember: people who don't look the part are cast as NSFU – *not suitable for upgrade* – and consigned to steerage hell.

REAL-LIFE BLAGGER

Anna Anderson: phoney princess

This fake Russian royal blagged travel, fame and fortune by convincing academics and European royals that she was Anastasia, the Romanov princess reputed to have been executed alongside the Russian royal family in 1918. The fact she was born in Poland and couldn't speak Russian didn't stop people believing the Russian royal escapee story. She received donations from Russian expats, toured the world and eventually married a wealthy American. After her death, DNA tests proved she was a fake.

How to get a discount on your air fare

Be a courier ...
... of documents, not drugs. When you carry documents on behalf of international businesses, you'll be paid by way of a discount on your air fare.

You have to be over eighteen, smartly dressed (this is a job, after all) and arrange your own visa where necessary. The best discounts from the UK are to New York and Japan in winter.

Be warned. If you cancel after booking a job, you're liable for the full economy air fare.

Contact the International Association of Air Travel Couriers (*www.aircourier.co.uk*). You need to become a member, which costs around £30 and doesn't suit everyone, but it could save you hundreds of pounds on your tickets.

Avoid spontaneity
Cheap tickets sell fast. If you want to seduce a prospective lover on the cheap, whisper in their ear: 'How do you fancy going away on the third Tuesday of the month after next, travelling from Bournemouth at four in the morning?'

If you're prepared to be this precise, prices tumble. Love is about commitment, after all.

Or leave it till the last minute
Aeroplane seats are the ultimate perishable goods. Once the plane is airborne, every spare seat is lost income to the airline. The best time to haggle is in the few minutes before a flight closes.

Get yourself bumped and fly for free

Because many passengers don't turn up for their flights – particularly business travellers, or others with flexible tickets – airlines often overbook flights, sometimes by as much as a third.

When they get their sums wrong, they're left with too few seats and too many travellers.

Make your reservation for flights that are most likely to be full

Peak holiday times, especially weekends; or early-morning and teatime flights to European business destinations are generally very busy, particularly on Mondays and Fridays. You're taking a bit of a gamble here – fares on these flights are often more expensive. Business people need to get to their meetings, and will not want to be the ones to give up their seats. Here's where you step in.

Offer to help the airline ...

When it's clear the airline is overbooked, find a representative and offer to be bumped off the flight. Arrive at the gate early and ask if they need volunteers. You may get a bumper bounty before it's offered to anyone else.

... or hold out for a bigger payout

If not enough people give up their seats, the airline will be forced to bump people who want to fly. It's bad for their reputation and is something they avoid. So as take-off time approaches, the bump offer gets bigger.

Don't hassle the gate attendants

Once you've volunteered, sit near the gate where they can find you easily. Checking the flight status every couple of minutes, especially when they are busy, won't encourage them to pay you a bigger bribe. Airline employees put up with a lot of aggro – and consequently they do a good line in spite.

But if you do manage to get bumped, airlines will be very nice to you indeed. Even though they're not obliged to, they'll put a bit of cash in your pocket, possibly give you a ticket for your next flight and, if you have to wait overnight, put you up in a posh airport hotel. If your rescheduled flight is later the same day, insist on going in the airline's executive lounge.

The biggest payout is when they are desperate for volunteers, of course. With luck, your flight will be rearranged to another overbooked slot and you can play the game all over again.

REAL-LIFE BLAGGER

Charles McKinley: cargo conman

Don't want to pay for an airline ticket? Send yourself freight and get your firm to pay, like Charles McKinley, who travelled freight-class from New York to Dallas. He went 1,500 miles in a box by lorry, plane and delivery van, before springing out of the box on his parents' doorstep.

Sadly, the delivery driver grassed on him, and he ended up with a fine, a year's probation and four months' house arrest. It could have been much worse: McKinley was fortunate to be placed in a pressurised, heated cabin.

How to get to your seat in comfort

Beat the rush. Bag more space in the overhead lockers and get the crew waiting on you before everyone else has sat down. To board ahead of the masses, you will need:

- Children (so find some).
- A disability (you may need some props to fake it).
- Someone to drive you.

The childish approach to boarding

The very old and the very young get preferential treatment on planes. If you're any age in between, and not accompanying anyone in this favoured category, you'll need to lie to get ahead.

Borrowing a child at check-in allows you to board the plane first. You also get a free goodie-bag.

The child will need its own boarding pass, so offer to help out someone who appears to have dozens of kids running round their ankles and lots of luggage. They will be grateful for the assistance. A name tag is a useful aid to winning short-term custody.

Ditch the child once seated. Keep the goodie-bag.

The dodgy-leg blag

Although some airlines board wheelchair users after other passengers, it's worth the wait for the personal attention you'll enjoy.

An injured knee (or perhaps just a knee brace) on the day of travel will see you whisked to your gate in a wheelchair with a nice man to carry your luggage. You may even get a ride on one of those tank-like buggies that other passengers who have to walk three-quarters of a mile envy.

Explain that your leg needs to be propped up and the chances are you'll be allocated three adjacent seats to spread yourself out.

You'll be first off at the other end, where you can make the decision to repeat the trolley and bag-carrier routine, or do a runner (best avoided on the outward leg).

Do notify the airline in advance of your injury. Sound in pain. Better still, get someone else to call, while making sure your screams are heard in the background.

Bug buggie drivers

You don't necessarily need to be lame to take the airline for a ride. If you have checked bags into the hold, they won't take off without you.

So don't rush to the gate the second your flight is called, no matter how far you have to walk. Relax in duty-free and then, when they're getting more anxious for final passengers for the flight (that's when they start naming and shaming you on the tannoy, saying they're about to dump your luggage), approach a buggie and insist on a lift.

Don't look worried that you'll miss the flight. You'd be quite happy to wait for the next one, you just don't want to put them to the trouble, expense and delay of searching for your bags.

Sometimes, you're just so considerate.

How to be treated like a VIP

Use a title

Knighthoods and peerages are best, but even if you're just a doctor, announce it. And, if you're not, tell people you are anyway. Make sure it says 'Dr' on your credit card. On your flight tickets. On your hotel booking.

In the event of a disaster, say you're a Doctor of Philosophy. No one has ever needed a philosophy lecturer in an emergency.

The same goes if you're a professor. You'll be neither use nor ornament when the flight goes down, but the crew and ground staff will treat you well at other times.

Change your name by deed poll

It's better to be a Rothschild or Beauchamp than an Ecclesthwaite or Pratt. A prestigious last name could be yours for a few pounds when you change it by deed poll.

A legal document, a deed poll is the name for a contract that concerns only one person – you. The particular contract you need is called a Deed of Change of Name, and it commits you to three key actions. You are:

- Abandoning your old name.
- Committing to use your new name at all times.
- Requiring the rest of the world to address you by your new name.

As long as the deed poll is properly prepared and witnessed, it's a legally binding document. You can even complete all the legalities over the Internet (*www.ukdps.co.uk*). The new you is then recognised in law.

Buying a barony or other landed title

Buy some Scottish land and become a lord of the manor.

A landed title can be added to your passport, although not on the main page alongside your name. But because a manorial lordship is not an aristocratic title, you can't legitimately call yourself lord or lady. You are styled John Smith, Baron of Thingummy, and you'll be addressed only as Thingummy, and not Lord Thingummy. But that's still quite impressive.

As a Scottish feudal baron, your title goes on all legal documents, such as credit cards, passport, driving licence, and your status is recognised in law.

But beware. Some baronies don't come cheap. The Barony of Macdonald came on the market at £1 million in 2003.

The Manorial Society of Great Britain (*www.msgb.co.uk*) can help with the purchase, but charges 10 per cent of the cost of buying your title.

Other elite titles

You can call yourself whatever you want without paying, just by registering a trademark. Alternatively, elite titles come up for sale at modest prices and, although they don't come with land, they may be quite legitimate. However, bogus titles and fake lords abound, so take care where you buy from.

It may be more socially beneficial to get someone to nominate you for the House of Lords. In this age of democracy, they need all types.

Timing is everything

If you want to drive off in a posher car than you've paid for, arrive at the rental office at the crack of dawn. This is the time when they are short of economy cars because they haven't been brought back in yet from the previous day. You're more likely to get an upgrade.

REAL-LIFE BLAGGER

Matthew Richardson: long-distance lecturer

Mistaken for a New York university professor of the same name, this engineering student from Oxford took an all-expenses paid trip to China to lecture on global economics.

Having borrowed an A-level textbook, because he thought he would be teaching a bunch of sixth formers, to his horror Richardson was confronted with a conference hall full of boffins studying for PhDs. Luckily, he managed to blag his way through by reading aloud from the textbook. He was even told by students how informative his lectures were. During the second day of teaching, however, having finished the textbook, he did a runner.

How to get free booze at an airport

Lounge around

Almost all airports have executive lounges, where business travellers freshen up and get boozed up. You can be part of the club – in the UK or abroad.

A small fee and smart appearance gets you in. It's well worth the modest outlay, and if you're a member of an airline's frequent-flyer programme, it may be free. Once in the lounge, you don't have to pay for drinks or snacks, and it's well away from the hoi polloi. Even a short delay to your flight can make it profitable.

The Cyprus Airways lounge at Larnaca costs about £13, for example. A couple of drinks and a snack in the public bar may cost you almost as much. With check-in two hours before departure, chances are you're going to consume more than a couple of drinks.

What you're really paying for is luxury. To be away from people like you.

It's in the cards
Your credit card may be a passport to lounges across the world. Check the promotional extras that come with your card – use of airport lounges may be one of them. Diners Club members, for example, enjoy lounge access – but take care, as you usually have to pay for the card. Wait for a free offer before signing up.

Having already signed up for the frequent-flyer programme of every airline, check out the latest offers. You may be able to trade air miles for lounge access.

Make an announcement
In airport bars, discover the names of your fellow travellers by taking a peek at their luggage tags, just as they have ordered a round of drinks. Then ask the announcements desk to put out an urgent call for the drinkers – something along the lines of Mr and Mrs So-and-So should meet a representative from their travel company (the name of which is also on their luggage). Back at the bar, watch as the clueless travellers panic and rush off – leaving their drinks for you.

How to get free accommodation when you travel

Friends in hot places
Encourage friends to take jobs in exotic locations. Unless you ski, hot ones are best. Your aim is to have a friend in every desirable location around the world.

When you meet new people on your travels, store their home addresses carefully, preferably on a computer system that lets you track them by location, not name. Before you set off on a trip, check the database for anyone you know, however slightly. Everyone says, 'If you're ever in the area, we'd love to see you.' Test their sincerity.

Seek sanctuary
Saying you are a criminal on the run or, more plausibly, a refugee, could get you a free room for the night. In the Middle Ages, if you were on the run from the law, the Church would give you sanctuary. You may find some holy places that still adhere to it.

So become an outlaw. Monasteries make wonderful places for free bed and board, in beautiful surroundings – and with fresh honey in plentiful supply.

Go to interviews for jobs you don't want
Want to visit somewhere or fancy a night in a hotel? Simply look for jobs in the local area and apply for scores of them. If you have a carefully crafted CV, some employers will invite you for interview – but before you head off, make sure that they will pay for travel. Okay, so you have to go and sit in front of some people for half an hour and answer tedious questions, but that can be quite a laugh in itself, particularly if you have no interest whatsoever.

How to blag freebies at a hotel

Even a single overnight visit to a hotel should generate two bars of soap, two small bottles of shampoo, two of conditioner and two sewing kits. And, if you want them, two shower caps too. Taking the toiletries when you leave is not stealing. It's part of what you pay for when you stay in a hotel.

The washbag slip
To get double quotas, put the toiletries into your washbag before you go to breakfast. The cleaner then replaces everything.

When you return to your room, pack this new lot into your washbag too. Then complain that the cleaner has forgotten to leave fresh toiletries.

Beware. If you leave some unused, or very slightly used, they will be arranged nicely for you, but not necessarily replaced. This is wasteful.

One small bottle of shampoo should last you three or four mornings anyway. More if you're bald. By procuring toiletries in this way, you can go without buying soap, shampoo and conditioner for a considerable time. You need never buy any again if you travel regularly.

You won't get if you don't ask

All but the most basic hotels are there to serve you, rather than just provide a bed for the night. Many will provide further toiletries and extras like combs and toothbrushes, if you ask. If you want stationery, pencils, newspapers, they will usually try to help, and often don't charge.

Expect to pay for more extravagant requests, of course, but it may be worth it for the look on their faces. In the very top hotels, they're trained not to bat an eyelid to guests' exotic requests: musical instruments, pythons, an escort service, that sort of thing.

Your comments on file

Always complete the guest form in your room. Say you like the hotel, so you'll be back – though you were somewhat disappointed by the smutty movies on the TV channel, the lack of your favourite tipple in the minibar, and you thought you saw a rodent scurry across the floor. Taken together, this simply isn't good enough, but you thought you would politely mention it, so they can attend to these shortcomings. Add credibility to your complaint by asking the manager to congratulate particular employees who have made your stay rather special (namely those who have acceded to any of your demands).

Your comments should get you on the hotel's database, making an upgrade to a superior room, or some welcoming gift, more likely when you return.

The wrong type of room

When you pre-book a room, many hotels will ask you whether you require a smoking or non-smoking room, one with a bath or one with a shower. When you get to your room, insist that whatever you have been allocated is wrong. The hotel may try to correct you: 'It does say you wanted a smoking room, sir', at which point you tell them you stopped smoking eight years ago and you keep asking them to update their records.

The inference should be that it is their error, whatever the reservation slip says. If the hotel is full, they will have to upgrade you, perhaps to the business suite, where the drinks and breakfast are free. If there's no way of moving you and you have to put up with the room, you deserve a discount or a good dinner.

Tonight's the night

If you're on honeymoon – or you say that you are – or you tell the staff it's some other special occasion like an important anniversary, big birthday or the night that you intend to propose to your loved one, many hotels will go out of their way to make your night go to plan. They may smooth the way with a bottle of champagne, fresh flowers or even an upgrade.

How to blag a seat on a crowded train

If possible, catch a train at the start of its journey. The end of the line is the place with the most free seats. If this is impossible, a disguise is called for – and is easy to achieve.

Act blind to take advantage of people's good nature

If you'd offer a blind person your seat on a train, you're a fine upstanding citizen (but perhaps this book isn't for you, after all). Because most people would offer up their seat, it's the very reason you should act blind. You will need:

- A white stick.
- Dark glasses.
- A stack of Post-it notes.

This is a win-win blag. A social service. You get a seat. And you make others feel good about themselves.

Don't buy your ticket from a touch-screen machine and remember that consistency is essential if you travel the same route regularly. You cannot be blind one day, sighted the next. In your normal guise, you are as anonymous as the rest of us, but once you are seemingly blind, people will remember their acts of kindness – and turn to vengefulness if you're caught.

As you are unable to spend the journey reading, a nap is the most productive use of your time. Attach a pre-prepared sticky label to your forehead with the words 'Wake me up at Wimbledon' (or appropriate station). People will be only too glad to help.

The pregnant woman variation
Suitable for females only, this blag is best performed by fat women under forty-five.

If you qualify: do not ask for a seat. Stick out your stomach, arch your back and waddle slightly when you move. Then hold one hand protectively over your belly, while flicking through a 'mother and baby' magazine. You are more likely to be offered a seat by other women. Men fear the embarrassment of mistaking a pregnant woman for someone who is merely fat, inadvertently double-bluffing your blag.

If a pregnant woman offers you her seat, take it.

Two are better than one
One train seat is never really enough, especially if you want to spread out and relax. But to avoid rubbing up against other travellers, don't plonk a bag down on the seat next to you and resort to tired bluffs like staring out of the window or pretending to be asleep. Instead, as the passengers walk down the train looking for somewhere to park themselves, make eye contact, fix them with a sultry look and gently pat the seat beside you. No one wants to sit next to a letch.

What to do when someone asks for directions

What a coincidence!
If a motorist stops to ask directions, tell them you're headed to the same place – what a surprise – and suggest you jump in.

If they don't know where they're going, they won't know when they haven't got there. You get an unexpected lift to wherever you wanted to go.

Don't look insane or threatening when you do this one. They'll lock the doors and drive off. Be polite and, if they do rumble the ruse when you ask to be dropped off, shrug your shoulders and say you've made a mistake. Generally, you can point to a junction and tell them to take it. Then melt into your environment.

What's it worth?

We live in a knowledge economy. This means if you know something someone else doesn't, you have valuable information. So don't give information away, sell it. Use the law of supply and demand. The more desperate someone is (demand), and when you're the only person around for miles (supply), the more money you can extract.

You don't even need to know the way. A bit of 'left here, right at the lights, straight on at the roundabout' should earn you a couple of quid. More if you're very polite and smile lots. When you're taking the money, smiles will come naturally.

Expect many people to drive off in a huff – but what's that to you? You haven't lost anything. If they're really in need, or just going round in circles, they'll be back.

REAL-LIFE BLAGGER

François Rabelais: package tourer

When fifteenth-century satirical writer Rabelais found himself stranded at a country inn with no money to continue his journey to Paris, poison appeared to be the answer. The quick-thinking author made up three small packets – 'Poison for the King', 'Poison for the Landlord', and 'Poison for the Prince' – and left them in clear view of the innkeeper, who not unnaturally called the police. Rabelais was bundled into a carriage and taken to Paris for questioning. There the police realised the packets were empty and released the happy traveller into the city to which he'd been heading.

How to cross a busy road

The advantage of your own zebra crossing

Forget the Green Cross Code. Everywhere is a safe place to cross when you own a portable zebra crossing, which can be unravelled wherever you want to cross. A Japanese invention that you can buy over the Internet, it's made of plastic and, as it's painted with black and white stripes, it works perfectly well in Europe.

Hold a quick demo

You have a right to protest – but not to hold up the traffic. However, experience shows the traffic doesn't know its rights: it will stop if you hold up a placard.

Get one in the shape of a lollipop with 'STOP: Children' written on it.

Push a pushchair

Child not necessary. Considerate drivers, and even the less-considerate but socially responsible ones who would happily mow down a bunch of teenagers, will slow down for parents with a pushchair or pram. It is a useful accessory for short trips where you have to negotiate a big junction. Take one when you go out for your morning paper – the streets are full of pushchairs at that time and no one will suspect.

How to blag the best space on the beach

Getting to the beach first isn't always desirable if you want to spend a leisurely morning at your hotel or apartment before stretching out by the sea. Blag your space in advance.

Make the best spots less appealing

- Erect 'Danger: treacherous tides, do not bathe' signs near the nicest bathing water.
- Leave things like fake turds or empty syringes lying around. (Make sure the needles have been removed.)

- To deter young families, smoke strong cigarettes or, even better, a pungent cigar.
- Leave a tent up overnight while you go and party.
- Put lots of pebbles down to create your own pebble beach. Most people prefer sand and will search elsewhere. You pack the pebbles away when you turn up.

Be the family from hell

Once you have occupied your space, put off families from hell getting close to you – by being the family from hell. Think big. Think noise. Think yobs. Then, when everyone else has moved away, relax.

- Play loud, tuneless music – high beats-per-minute if you're trying to rid yourself of old people; classical music if you want rid of noisy youths.
- Take lots of inflatables.
- A huge windbreak will define your territory.
- An energetic game of bat and ball will warn off anyone thinking of parking their towel near yours.
- Build large sandcastles, with a moat that extends round your entire territory. This marks out your space clearly, provides a natural barrier that people will be reluctant to cross, and few will want to trample down a child's carefully constructed castle.

REAL-LIFE BLAGGER

Reverend Philip Waller: happy holy-daymaker

The saying goes that money doesn't buy you happiness, so one British vicar set out to prove it. Rocking reverend Philip Waller was awarded £1,300 to go clubbing and windsurfing and to spend three months in Africa, just to find out what makes people happy. An insurance firm and a religious-studies college paid for him to travel in search of happiness. He told reporters it wasn't a free holiday by any means: 'I want to find out why people in more affluent societies are generally more unhappy than those in poorer countries,' he said.

blagging it...
romance and sex

How to blag a kiss

If you want to succeed in dating, you must take every opportunity that presents itself. Start with stealing kisses wherever you can. Try these tips.

Fake illness or tragedy

Go for the sympathy vote. Say you've just discovered that you have a disease – one that probably isn't terminal, but, crucially, could be. A medical dictionary will help you swot up on symptoms to make your story authentic. Never make the disease a communicable one – no one will come near you.

When faking tragedy, don't go for a drama that can be uncovered easily – like the invented demise of a parent. It would take some explaining when you introduce them if things go further. Pretend a cherished pet has copped it, or an old friend has been killed while dabbling in an extreme sport in some faraway spot like Chile, so they're never likely to find a body.

Everyone needs a hug at times like these. Only someone with a heart of stone would deny you an embrace and a kiss when you are facing such trauma.

Exploit goodbyes

Snogging someone when you're introduced for the first time can cause alarm. Goodbyes are a different matter. The Continental custom of kissing on both cheeks is now commonplace. Go as if to make this gesture, then miss at the last second, landing a smacker full on your target's lips.

Your embarrassed apology should be accepted graciously – and it will be a talking point when you meet again.

Clean up with kissing customs

On 'Kissailing Day', it's traditional to snog strangers. Americans in particular think British customs are quaint, so you could achieve a high-smacker rate in touristy areas. Of course, Kissailing Day doesn't exist – but it could. Create your own elaborate kissing custom for a special day.

National Kissing Day, on the other hand, is on 6 July every year and really does exist (it was invented, incidentally, by a dental insurance company, the blaggers). Alternatively, take someone for a country walk through lots of 'kissing gates'.

New Year's Eve is a gift for seeking out snogs. If you haven't had a kiss all year, the stroke of midnight is the time to grab a guest or ravish a reveller. And during December, carry mistletoe everywhere you go. Whip it out whenever you can.

Holiday in kissing hotspots

When planning a trip abroad, make sure that the culture is inclined to liberal snogging. On the Côte d'Azur, take advantage of the local custom for a five-or six-peck marathon when greeting someone. Better still, visit Pays de Mont in Brittany where a kiss called the *Maraichinage* was invented – a snog that lasts for hours.

Your chances of blagging a snog are almost non-existent in some places. In South America some tribes don't believe in kissing at all, and in Africa, one tribe, the Thonga, are disgusted by the 'Western' practice of kissing on the lips. But then, they do have a point. There are said to be more germs in the mouth than in the anus.

Take up amateur dramatics

Organise your own theatre group, and play the romantic lead every time. Choose dramas with intimate scenes like *Romeo and Juliet*, *Casablanca* or that famous romance *No Sex Please, We're British*. You get to snog the leading actor of the opposite sex.

How to blag a sexual encounter

You work in a sexy profession
Some people are prepared to sleep their way to success, the cads. Use this fact and by the time your prey discovers you're lying, it's all too late.

Sexy jobs include:

- TV director – they think you'll put them on telly.
- Movie producer – even better. An excuse for you to get them to take their clothes off – 'for the camera test'.
- Surgeon – try the chat-up line: 'I'd love to take you to dinner – but first a small medical.'
- Struggling artist – so bohemian, and a chance to be cheap at the same time.
- Nurses, firemen, police officers: any job that needs a uniform is a top turn-on.
- Lawyers, bankers and other professions. According to a Top Totty survey by recruitment website Fish4Jobs, people look far sexier in suits than in casual clothes.

Never say:

- I just work in an office.
- I work on the bins.
- I've just come out of prison.

Play with your sexuality
The idea that their partner has slept with someone of their own sex can be a turn-on for both men and women. Heterosexual men, dubbed 'Strays' – STRaight gAYS – pretend to be gay in order to pull women. It really works – women don't feel they're going to get pulled. Big mistake.

Follow hens and stags
When out on the town, look for girls on a hen night or boys on a stag do.

They're always up for a bit more fun and desperate to have a story to tell at the coming wedding reception.

Be racially aware

It's simple – some races have more sex. So increase your chances: date someone from the Aranda aborigines in Australia who, according to anthropologists, have sex five times a night.

Heavy petting

Buy a dog and you will find more people stop and talk to you. Walk alone and people think you're strange. Walk with a Dobermann and they'll freeze. Walk an Alsatian and they'll run away. Choose something pattable, but not too silly. A sheepdog, rather than a King Charles spaniel.

Borrow a kid

Men could take a leaf out of Nick Hornby's bestselling book, *About A Boy*. Offer to take a friend's kid out for the afternoon – it'll help you enter into casual conversation with women who may be attracted by your caring and lovable nature. Reveal that the child isn't yours early on in your conversation to make it clear that you're available.

REAL-LIFE BLAGGER

Cheryl Bevan: phone-a-fiancé

Swansea-girl Cheryl Bevan bagged the man of her dreams when she dialled the wrong number and ended up with a new husband. After splitting up from her former husband, Cheryl was trying to phone a friend but misdialled and got through to legal consultant Geoff Thorrington, 150 miles away in Devon. She chatted him up and within three months they were living together. They married the following year.

How to blag a long-lasting relationship

Embarrass them into staying with you

Find out sensitive details about your partner's life that they don't want anyone to know, or ingratiate yourself with their parents so that their family has an emotional investment in your relationship. It will then be hard for your partner to break their hearts too.

The money's on its way

Make yourself look rich. Mention wealthy dying relatives, mythical inheritances and share options. This is especially attractive to anyone already paying a big mortgage or hoping to own their own home, or quite simply looking for someone to provide an extravagant lifestyle. If they're going to take you on for life, they want to know there's going to be lots in it for them.

Compile a lonely-hearts ad

No need to embarrass yourself by telling the truth.

To attract a woman (if you're a man):

- State your salary (it's big).
- Allude to your height (you're tall).
- Mention your looks (unnervingly handsome).
- Talk about your hair (you have some).
- A word about your interests (music, dining out, exotic holidays are safe; porn and pubs are not).
- You're looking for commitment.

To attract a man (if you're a woman):

- Outline your employment status (you either wear a uniform, or you're rich enough not to work).
- Mention your looks (glamorous, attractive).
- State what you seek in a man (modesty and humour – you won't

get it, of course, but you'll maximise the number of people replying).
- Be clear about your intentions (good sex is important, marriage isn't. Once you've trapped them, you can work on what you really want).

Tell the right lies

Don't be ashamed of telling lies. The right lies are essential to long-lasting relationships.

Men should always lie when women ask ...

- Does my bum looks big in this?
- Am I better looking than your ex?
- Do you fancy her?

Women should always lie when men ask ...

- Is it big?
- Do you like my car?
- Am I the best lover you've ever had?

It pays to advertise

Someone, somewhere is desperate enough to go out with you. You just need to find them – and the Internet can help. You don't have to be good looking, and you can manipulate your looks by posting a false picture, or touching-up a real one. When you finally meet your date, they may be disappointed with the real thing, but now's your chance to show off your great personality. Normally, of course, they wouldn't have given you a second look.

Keep them in the dark

Worried about your looks? Try dating in the dark, an organised event where you meet your date at an unlit restaurant. The waiters wear night vision goggles and the menu is strictly finger food. Check out *www.dinnerinthedark.com*.

How to save money on your date

'But it's so romantic ...'

Cut costs by convincing the one you fancy to do something wacky and, most importantly for you, cheap.

Save money on a hotel by suggesting you spend the night in a tent under the stars, or make a fire and sleep on the beach. Other simple and cheap date ideas include reading to each other and, of course, picnics.

Cook for two on the cheap

While steak and posh fish dishes can break the bank – and let's face it, after all that effort they might still not deliver the goods – your garden is a source of fancy food that would cost a fortune in a restaurant. An exotic dish is closer to home than you might think.

So cook woodpigeon or even grey squirrel. All are easily found in your garden, and the cat can help with the kill. Bear in mind that in a restaurant, woodpigeon can set you back as much as £30 a bird – and they're really skinny. Your partner won't know whether you've cooked them the right way or not and they'll be impressed with your adventurous talents. However, don't expect them to eat it all. For inspiration, try *www.seasonalfood.com*.

Make it like the movies

Recreate a movie scene – one that allows you to be cheap, but still shows your mushy side. You could sit in a railway café all day and imagine you're in *Brief Encounter*. Or tell your partner that it would be romantic to recreate *Breakfast at Tiffany's* where Audrey Hepburn and George Peppard spend the day doing things they haven't done before – including buying the cheapest gift at the famous jewellery store (these days it's a refill for a Tiffany's propelling pencil).

Even pizza can be romantic

You want to take them out for a memorable and romantic meal, but don't want to shell out. Call a cheap pizza place before you go on the date and arrange for your pizza to be cut into a heart shape before it's delivered to your table. Many restaurants will do this for nothing.

How to choose inexpensive gifts for the ones you love

Don't splurge on expensive gifts. After all, there's nothing sweeter than giving something cheaper. Blag it ...

Flowers

Pick your blooms from your garden or windowbox, or buy a single red rose – romantic and so much cheaper than the full dozen.

Make it yourself

The only cost is time – and how can your partner criticise something that was made especially for them? Make a tape of your favourite love songs. All it costs is the blank cassette or CD – less than a pound – and it's free when you record over something else.

When it comes to cards, get a silly or romantic photo of yourself or your partner, cut it out and stick it on a piece of card with a funny caption. Melts them like butter.

Sexy lingerie
Women should buy it before their men get round to it. He'll think it's a present to him. Best of all, you then don't have to wear the naff stuff he chooses.

Better still, skimp on sexy underwear by never wearing any. Men will forget about the frilly stuff completely when you slip this into a conversation. For added thrills, make the announcement in a public place.

Prey on family sentimentality
Ask grandparents, aunties and uncles if they have any antique rings that you can use as an engagement ring or wedding band, or rummage round junk shops till you come across something that looks authentic. Tell your partner that it is a family heirloom. Antique rings can be cheaper than new ones and usually look just as good.

Write a love letter ...
... but get an expert to do it by using an Internet love-letter generator. Or go to the library and cobble together your own love poem from bits of others. Unless they've got a degree in English Literature, they'll never twig.

How to blag the most out of dating

Too many relationships end in premature failure. So get as much out of your dating as possible while the going is good.

Use a date to get a date
If you're honest, perhaps you don't fancy them enough, but date someone who has the right contacts and they could lead you to the perfect partner. For example, you might date a gaffer to get to a film director, a receptionist to date a stockbroker, or a butler for a taste of upper-class life.

You're never more attractive than when you're unavailable. So a romantic date is the perfect time to call up old flames who dumped you and gloat that you've found true love. They'll be much more likely to want to date you all over again.

Dump at the right time of year

Most relationships break down after important occasions like Christmas
or Valentine's Day. It's important to make sure you don't dump your
partner before these dates, or just before your own birthday, because
you want the presents. Of course, you don't want to go to the expense
of giving anything (other than the elbow), so dump them just after your
partner has given you your gift but before you hand anything over.

Flash a ring

Flirt while wearing a wedding ring (easier if you're married; a useful
accessory to carry, if not) and tempt the opposite sex into doing
something naughty. They know that it's likely to be just a one-night stand,
giving you the perfect excuse to walk away.

How to blag your way out of a relationship

As Paul Simon wisely explained, there are fifty ways to leave your lover.
Follow his advice. Blag it by making them think they dumped you. These
tips will grind them down until they've had enough. Not only do you win
your freedom, you get the chance to look all hurt too.

Tips for women:

- Re-arrange his alphabetically ordered CDs. When he sorts them out
  again, muck them up straight away.
- Criticise his choice of car (tell him his sporty two-seater is a
  'hairdresser's car').
- Laugh loudly at his mates' jokes. When he cracks a gag, look
  baffled.
- Copy his disgusting behaviour. Hog the remote control, drink too
  much and fart in bed.
- Talk about your hopes for a large family.

Tips for men:

- Always leave the toilet seat up. And miss. Every time.
- Criticise her driving, clothes and her hair.
- Criticise anything else she's sensitive about.
- Then deny you're criticising her. You were just trying to help.
- Give her the silent treatment. Women hate it when men refuse to argue back.
- Subtly ridicule bits of her body. You might say, 'You've got a stray hair there, darling,' looking at her chin. Of course she already knows about it. Then feign innocence.
- Try the 'What on earth is that smell!' just after she's put on perfume.

How to blag your way through a cut-price affair

Adultery can be an expensive sin. Use these tips to justify your infidelity.

Secrecy costs less
If you're going to play around, conceal what you're doing by sticking to old habits. Fuse savings and secrecy like this:

- Tell them you can't go for a meal out or treat them to expensive gifts because it will alert your respective other halves. You can't be expected to pay for anything at all, in fact, because it will show up on your credit-card bill. Explain that it's safer if your lover pays as your spouse checks your receipts – you don't want such tell-tale evidence falling out of purses, wallets or clothes. Oh, and you never carry much cash.

- Remember – you car's back seat is cheaper than a hotel. Even better, your lover's back seat is cheaper and you save on cleaning bills. Under no circumstances should you shell out on a hotel room when vehicles are free and more exciting.

- Don't bother spending money on lipstick as tell-tale kiss marks have to be avoided at all costs (or rather, no cost).

Target older people
Maturer men and women won't expect to be impressed with posh dinners and expensive gifts if you're much younger than them. They'll be in it for the sex and, of course, that's free. Not only that, they'll be eager to shower *you* with gifts when you're their toyboy or trophy girlfriend.

Combine an affair with business
Have an affair with your client. If they're sleeping with you, they will want to give you more business (and, if they don't, blackmail is always an option). Alternatively, if you're someone's boss, exploit your position by becoming your subordinate's lover. They'll be afraid to make too many demands – after all, their job depends on you.

How to date a celebrity

Top celebrities constantly complain that their celebrity status means they can't find love. Hollywood hunk George Clooney once claimed that only his pot-bellied pig really understood him. The rich and famous are often ripe for overtures from people who can rescue them from life in the spotlight. Here's how to cosy up to the stars.

Choose the right celebrity
Avoid really well-known mega-celebrities, they are overburdened with nutters. Write instead to reality-TV stars offering to be their agent, or say that you have some unique service to offer them such as celebrity baby-care or privacy management. Aspiring models are also worth targeting, as they won't cost you much in food bills.

You're a bigger star than they are
Celebs stick together to avoid falling for 'kiss-and-tell' honey traps. So worm your way into a VIP party (see page 120), then act like you're the biggest star in the room. When you're introduced to a celeb, make them feel that they should be grateful that they have your time and attention.

Exude confidence, indifference, mystery. They will be too embarrassed to ask why you're famous (but if they do, you could be a top writer or renowned architect), and, as part of the fame club, you're safe to date.

If matters do progress further, kiss and tell.

Become a roadie

Get a part-time job as something that will bring you into contact with celebs but that doesn't make you look like an obsessed fan. Be a driver, bodyguard or make-up artist.

Or a groupie

Traditionally, after a rock gig, horny young women are much in demand by animalistic musicians (and their friends). The rise of 'girl power' creates just as much opportunity for male groupies. And if you're a country-music fan, age is no barrier.

Standing like a drip with your autograph book won't get you noticed. Take your top off, provide a felt-tip and ask them to sign parts of your anatomy. Some traditions should never die.

The benefits of getting hitched

Not for the faint-hearted, because this can actually cost you money. But if you think that the hazards of marriage will be offset by the financial benefits it brings, it's worth a punt.

But first, check that:

- If you're a man, the bride's parents are rich enough to stand you a good party.
- If you're a woman, he's sure to take you on the honeymoon of your dreams.

If the answer to either of these is yes, it's worth a go.

Remember the sage advice: always get married in the morning. Then if things don't work out, at least you haven't wasted the whole day.

Rings of champagne

It may be romantic to present a ring at the point of proposal, but it's more profitable to shop for diamonds together. The more salubrious establishments ply prospective partners with champagne as they mull over expensive stones.

Indeed, why bother getting engaged at all? Window-shopping for engagement rings – without buying, of course – is the perfect way to get squiffy on someone else's champagne. Thursday and Friday nights are best: if you're in London, try the jewellery hotspots around Hatton Garden and Knightsbridge.

Wine dressing

Find out which bridal outfitters oil your decision with decent wine. Dressing up and getting drunk is a nice way to spend a Saturday afternoon. No wedding necessary.

Wed before you die

If you already own a house with your partner, but you're not married to them, you could leave a gigantic inheritance tax bill if you snuff it. This may not concern you (as you'll be dead), but just think what a headache you'll face if your partner drops first.

If you're worth more than about £285,000 – including the value of your house – the survivor is going to have to fork out 40 per cent of the remainder to the government. You may have to sell the house to pay the bill.

So the moment you vaguely feel like death could be close, get married. An inheritance-tax wedding may not be romantic, but it is practical.

The prezzies

It's traditional for guests to buy you gifts to set you up in your new home. The quid pro quo is that you throw a massive party. Set some ground rules:

- You only have a party if someone else – like your parents – pays.
- You want money in lieu of gifts – so you can put a value on your friendships.

Reduce the risk of presents you don't want. Choose your wedding list from an expensive shop. Include several cheap items to make it appear that you have given people the option to buy small, then buy these yourself immediately. Everyone will then think they've left it too late and plump for an expensive gift from the list out of necessity.

REAL-LIFE BLAGGER

Ganna Walska: singing serial bride

Walska was a crafty Polish-born woman who, early in the twentieth century, took up opera to attract the attention of the second-richest man in Russia – and married him. She went on to amass a fortune by marrying and divorcing another five gullible guys. Although she was not much of an opera singer, the money she garnered from her wealthy husbands helped her to establish her own fantasy gardens, called Lotusland, in Santa Barbara, California.

How to do your wedding on the cheap

Danger! Weddings can be one of the costliest things you'll ever do. So whether you're planning nuptials for your own big day or you're a parent expecting to shell out big time, these tips could help.

Cut costs on the frock

Some places specialise in only-worn-once dresses and other used wedding garments. Most bridal gowns have only been used on one day – so how badly worn can they be? After the event, you should store your dress carefully in case you marry again.

If you want something that looks like it's designer-made, take a magazine cutting of something you fancy and ask a local dressmaker to copy it. It will look the part at a fraction of the designer cost. Alternatively, contact the designer of your dream dress directly, rather than buying through a store. Many are one-man bands and will strike a deal when you cut out the middleman.

Love is worth more than trinkets ...

... so spurn the commercialism that has invaded the wedding ceremony. In 2003 the cost of the average wedding in the UK was £16,000. That's a lot of lolly to waste on a fancy-dress party.

Cut the cost of the rings by using comedy ones – they worked perfectly well in the first service in *Four Weddings and a Funeral*. However, forget to tell your fiancé what you're planning for the big day and it could be *your* funeral.

Tell your partner that success in marriage is in inverse proportion to the cost of a wedding. There's no need for wedding rings when all you need is love.

Look to your mother

Many women hold on to their wedding dresses all their lives without ever wearing them again. Ask the females of the family if they still have theirs. Your mum could well have been about the same size as you when she got married. And she'll appreciate the sentimental request.

'Something borrowed'

Borrow and beg from mates. By tradition, the bride is supposed to wear 'something borrowed' – this is a simple extension. You could ask a musical friend to organise a band or DJ for the disco. Get a relative who is good with a camera to take the wedding snaps. An alternative is to provide disposable cameras for everyone and ask for them to be left behind at the end – or get the guests to pay for developing and printing and send you a spare set. Everything costs less than hiring the professionals and gives your wedding the personal touch.

Sidestep Saturdays

You get better rates if you have a wedding on any other day but Saturday. Choose a day in the middle of the week – avoiding Mondays and Fridays, which guests may use to make a long weekend. You'll end up with fewer people to cater for. Tell them a present in lieu of attendance will do.

Tie the knot somewhere unusual

You can marry pretty much anywhere. Getting hitched at a department store, motorway service station or even a monkey sanctuary could land you with useful sponsorships or freebies. Themed weddings, such as a movie bash that ties in with the latest release, could also garner gifts and money from the film company. You could also sell your story to a magazine.

Flowers on the church

If you organise your wedding around religious festivals such as Easter or Christmas, when the church is already decorated, you save on the cost of flowers. Alternatively, get children to pick flowers and bring them along.

Open a honeymoon account

It's a fact of modern life that by the time most couples get married, they already have the gifts that traditionally would launch them in a new home. Follow the inspirational lead set by four out of ten newlyweds by getting guests to stump up for your honeymoon instead. Make a list of all the things you want to do and put a price against each one for your friends to set their names against.

REAL-LIFE BLAGGER

Andrea Nies: bluffing bride

A bride who didn't want to splash out on her wedding ditched the traditional white dress for one made out of an old shower curtain. Despite making good money from their jobs, both Andrea, a gynaecologist, and her husband wanted to save money on their big day. Her mum made up the dress and Andrea said she felt really special wearing it.

blagging it...
with the kids

How to blag your way through pregnancy and parenthood

Parents shell out over £20,000 bringing up a child to the age of five. It's money better spent on you. So save cash during pregnancy and the early years. Here's how.

Don't drop first

Timing is everything if you want to save the fortune it costs to kit out a kid. If you're in your fertile years, with friends of much the same age, wait until a few of them have started their families. By the time your child arrives they will be bending over backwards to clear out their homes by giving you their kids' cast-off clothes and toys.

If by some misfortune, you mistime your own happy event, sell your cast-offs through the classifieds before your friends come blagging.

With or without?

It pays to find out the sex of your baby early. Pregnancy takes time, prices are going up, and you don't want to miss the sales while you wait. Some say it's romantic to be surprised. It's not: it's simply uneconomic.

Reproduce in a profitable place

If your waters break in a major department store, many will consider sending you a special baby gift pack. Hang around an expensive shop on the date you're due to drop.

For a lifetime of free flying, give birth on a generous airline. Your new child may also benefit from dual nationality. You could certainly make a claim, depending on which airspace the baby was born in (you could say you have an Icelandic child, for example, if you give birth mid-air between the UK and US).

Help granny bond

Why pay for childcare when grandparents come free? It's good for baby and grandparents to bond early by spending time together. Also, when showing the newborn to your friends, hand the baby over while saying: 'Say hello to your Uncle (or Auntie) Such-and-such.' You may lose a friend, but gain a babysitter.

Toys Я Useless

Toddlers don't value expensive toys, even if you do. They much prefer saucepan lids or car keys. Show that you truly dote on their desires by giving them such cheap entertainment. However, there is no need to deny your child expensive toys. Friends and relatives will want to give baby presents, and when they ask what they should buy, be quick to name something pricey.

Also, babies don't know if they're wearing nice new clothes or not. So dress them in any old stuff. And never buy baby shoes. The baby needn't be shod until it has made the effort to walk properly.

REAL-LIFE BLAGGER

Anette Lie: breast-milk blagger

A Norwegian woman who has sold over 500 litres of her breast milk bought a car with the income. Anette Lie was paid £11 per litre and made a total of £5,275, milking her clients for every penny she could.

She says her ability to produce so much milk is genetic. 'My mother was the same way, and I've heard my grandmother nursed children around town, so it's hereditary. It's my hormones. I apparently have lots of them.'

Give your child a name that opens doors

Call me 'Sir'

By giving your child a title as their first name, you provide a gift that lasts a lifetime – and it's perfectly possible to do. The law says that you must give your child at least a first name and a surname, so why not make the first one Sir or Baron or Dame? The baby doesn't even need to have the same last name as either of its parents, so instead of Sarah Jones, how about Lady Farqharson? Their titled first name will appear on the child's passport and, later, their credit card and job application to a well-heeled corporation. When they fill out a form, or are introduced at a reception, they will be Dame Britney or Lord Justin.

If you have made the mistake of registering your offspring without a 'Sir' or 'Earl' or 'Princess' as a first name, the bad news is that you can't change it later by deed poll. Titled names are only allowed when registered at birth.

Pick the right initials

Choose David Richard, Daisy Rebecca, Daniel Russell or Diane Ruth and your child can go through life looking, from the name on their credit card, as if they are a doctor. Years of training unnecessary.

For boys, Simon Ian Richard or Stewart Ivan Ruben will make it look to the uninitiated as if your son has been knighted.

REAL-LIFE BLAGGER

Prince:

Until he changed his name to a squiggle and back again, Prince called himself Prince. Incidentally, he wouldn't have got away with the squiggle ploy in the UK, where unpronounceable names aren't allowed. Worse, he wouldn't have been able to call himself Prince. British birth certificates demand a first name and a last name. Prince alone isn't acceptable. But Prince Prince would be okay.

How to choose a gullible godparent

You might not be able to choose your family, but when it comes to godparents, pragmatism means presents. The rule is simple. Rich is best.

Selecting a godparent for your child has nothing to do with religion or who your best friends are, but everything to do with gift potential.

Ideally, godparents provide a child with a different perspective on life from your own. A great godparent should be a giver.

You are a taker.

Traps to avoid:

- Don't choose close relatives – they can reasonably be expected to contribute to your child's wealth and toy collection anyway.
- Don't confine the role to a ceremonial one: make it clear you expect the active giving of time (money needn't be mentioned).
- Don't choose a friend on the basis of the many boozy evenings you've enjoyed together. You're about to ask them to renounce the Devil and handle your dribbling offspring. You need to sell the job.

The perfect godparent:

- Is rich. This goes without saying.
- Is loyal. This person is expected to provide a lifetime's commitment.
- Doesn't come to stay overnight.
- Takes your kids on trips, removing the need for you to spend your own money entertaining the children.
- Changes nappies.
- Is so flattered to be asked, takes the parents out for an expensive meal.
- Does not need to like children. Indulging them is the sole requirement.
- Knows that holidays – or holy-days, as they were once known – were made for godparents to spend with godchildren, so you don't need to go along.
- Knows the value of a private education – and is prepared to pay.

- Should not have children of their own. This makes yours all the more special. Catch someone in their twenties and you can have ten years' profitable godparenting out of them before their own kids come along. People in their forties who are never going to reproduce should also be considered.

Remember also, there is no rule about how many godparents you can choose for your child. The more you have, the more your child receives.

Open a savings account for your child
Godparents should be expected to provide expensive presents, leaving you to find stocking fillers – or, preferably, nothing. If the present your child really wants is cheap, buy it yourself and suggest the godparent puts money into the child's savings account.

Open a child's account which allows you to draw from it. Tell the kid it's for his holiday. Better still, don't tell the child about the account.

Everyone is a godparent
Heed the old African saying: 'It takes a whole village to raise a child.'

If the whole village will raise your child, hand it over.

How to profit from your children

Babies are notoriously costly. Get your money back. Exploit your kid.

Be a pregnant guinea pig
Baby and toddler magazines offer mums-to-be road tests on all kinds of baby products. Tell them about your happy event the second you get pregnant and offer to go on their testing panels. Loads of freebies will come your way.

Put them to work at once
Catalogue companies and advertisers need a constant flow of photogenic children. They don't even need to be able to act, talk or even walk. You can make money out of them from the day they're born and often before, as some agencies represent pregnant women.

You'll need the help of a reputable child modelling agency. There are many bogus ones waiting to part you from your money, so check them out thoroughly. Look at their agency book which shows the kids they represent. Ask to see copies of work that children on their books have done and check that it matches the photos of the kids in their portfolio.

Christenings and baby showers

Do have a christening – even if you're not religious. If you choose a secular naming ceremony, beware – surprisingly, some people think these bashes are only for trendy environmentalists who spurn commercialism. As this reduces the gift quota, assure people it isn't true.

Hold a baby shower at work to get presents from people you don't want anywhere near your home life.

Give your child a long name which is difficult to engrave on small christening gifts. Larger presents are guaranteed.

REAL-LIFE BLAGGER

Louise Carr: free delivery

Carr gave birth in the car park of a Heinz factory and was given a year's supply of baby food by the firm for her trouble. The thirty-year-old was leaving work at the site in Lancashire when her waters broke. Two nearby factory workers helped deliver the baby, who was five weeks early. The moral is: forget a home birth, plan factory reproduction if you want freebies.

Your baby is your bond

In the UK, every newborn child born gets a £250 gift – a 'baby bond' – stuck in a savings account by the government. Encourage your child to learn to write – and practise their signature on a contract pledging their money to you. When they're eighteen and can cash in their bond, tell them the stork flew off with it. After all, £250 is £250. The baby could well be the richest member of the family and will never have done a day's graft in its life. That can't be right.

Remember, the more children you have, the more money you get. Your child benefit is boosted too.

A surprise coming-of-age gift

On your child's eighteenth birthday, present them with an invoice for all the things you have done for them. They are unlikely to be impressed with a single request for the £100,000+ you have spent, so itemise everything as they go through life: 'one pair of football boots/ballet shoes per year for 12 years, at £35 a pair is £420'. It all mounts up.

As they enter their twenties, they are going to be inundated with bills: university fees, deposit for a house and so on. Your invoice can be their introduction to this world. It's for their own good.

Homework beyond their years

Do your kids' homework for them if you want them to succeed. If you don't understand it or can't be bothered, get an older child to do it for the younger ones. Their glory will reflect on you, they will get a better job and earn more money to keep you in your dotage.

If you build up a bank of good homework, sell it on the Internet or to other parents. There's a ready market for essays.

How to blag the kind of child you want

Get the right genes

For the most beautiful bouncing baby, buy the eggs and sperm of top models – all legal and online at sites like *www.ronsangels.com*. It's not quite cloning, but even if you just use one half of the mixture, you increase your chances considerably of having a child you'd want to look at.

Start education in the womb

The Jesuits said: 'Give me the child of seven and I will show you the man.' Far too late, of course. Instead, indoctrinate the unborn baby so that you mould the offspring of your dreams:

Sounds

Babies remember sounds from the womb and prefer whatever music they had to put up with before they made it to the outside. So if you want your kid to share your taste in 1970s punk rock, then whack up the volume on the sound system before birth. If you're hoping for an encyclopaedic knowledge of Mozart, play the classics.

Food
Babies prefer the flavours they first tasted in the womb, through mum's amniotic fluid. This can be used to stop them craving chips later on.

Expectant mothers who crave chocolate, though, end up with happier babies, according to Finnish researchers. The child is also more likely to stay calm and relaxed in new situations – except at the supermarket checkout where demands for chocolate are at their height. So eat more chocolate. You now have the perfect excuse – a happy, calm baby (and eventually, a spotty, obese teenager).

Invent a past
Make your children feel important by telling them spurious stories about their lineage. Convince them that they have famous ancestors and are members of the landed gentry. Buy cheap oil paintings of distinguished people to line your home, giving them the sense that they belong to a family of achievers. Your children will be eager to mix with posh kids, will seek high-paid jobs in dull industries and subsequently keep you in the style to which you want to be accustomed.

Marry a foreigner
The kids will grow up bilingual – but you never have to bother learning the language.

Or move abroad. The children get immersed in the language and you get a child of many tongues. As you won't be able to cope with the language, they can be your personal translators.

Start a school (for one)
Keep kids out of school if you want them to learn more. Children educated at home often do better in tests.

If they must go to a real school, make it a faith-based one, which tend to achieve better results. No need to get religion, of course. Just finish your Sunday morning walk by the church and shake the vicar's hand as he says goodbye to his congregation.

How to make money out of twins

Twins may be double trouble, but parents are entitled to dual child benefit. It's even better if you have triplets, quads or more.

As a package, twin births are cheaper than individual births; it gets the messy business of reproducing two children out of the way in one go, and doesn't interrupt your working life as much. Increase your chances by waiting until you're older and taking advantage of fertility treatments.

Teach your twins to act

TV and film companies need sets of identical children – even when their scripts call for only one kid. As young children tire easily, rules about their working hours are strict. Identical children can replace one another on the set, allowing filming to continue uninterrupted. (It's the same principle for Labrador puppies in Andrex commercials, which also tire easily – and find it hard to follow a script. Producers need a lot of dogs. So start a puppy farm.)

Check out *www.twinsworld.com* for a casting section that provides twins to the entertainment industry.

Twins are magic

Grown-up twins can continue their theatrical career, long after the calls from commercial directors have died away. Magicians crave twins. Particularly if one is a contortionist and can fold away whilst being sawn in half.

Get them running

Running a twenty-six-mile marathon is easier when two share the burden. True, to run even thirteen miles, they need to be quite fit, but if you train your twins early enough, there's money – and athletic fame – to be made in marathon running. They won't even need to run thirteen consecutive miles, providing there are sufficient places en route to mask a swap. Have a car on standby to rush the spare runner to the next switching point.

If you do decide to race them consecutively along the route, triplets or quads are preferred. If you're caught, say you thought it was a relay.

How to save money on presents and treats

Disguise their meals as take-aways

If chips from McDonald's or fried-chicken outings are treats in your family, reuse old boxes when presenting your kid's tea-time burger or chicken supper. They'll think you've splashed out just for them.

Exploit the power of imagination

Dressing-up boxes, an 'invention' box and your old rusty toolkit together make a decent and creative resource for your child's improvisation skills. As imagination is ruined by television (and, in particular, TV commercials), ban it without guilt and free yourself from pester-power.

Family 'present-opening' sessions

In general, young children are adored by your closest friends and relatives, who will be happy to send presents. Use this to ingratiate yourself into your toddler's affections further. Insist that they open Christmas and birthday presents one at a time in your presence – and pretend that they are from you. Hand each to the child with the happy remark: 'Here's another one from Mummy and Daddy' (or whoever you are in relation to said infant).

Get the child to write thank-you notes to people who haven't sent presents. It engenders guilt.

Buy big...
... but not necessarily expensive. Children like big presents. Put small ones in big boxes.

How to blag it at theme parks and attractions

Wear the right badge
Thousands of places accept the famous Blue Peter badges as currency. Win, borrow or fake one. It is recognised across the UK as proof that you have a good, talented or enterprising child.

Wear one yourself. Say you're a presenter of the programme. Or, if you're old, say you're a former presenter. No one remembers any of them except the ones they used to watch as a child.

'This place is famous!'
It costs surprisingly little to entertain very young children. Take them to a playground and tell them it's Disney World. When they're older, and badgering you to go, remind them that they've been before and didn't like it much.

Optimise the size of your group
If a theme park's family ticket allows two adults and up to three children, it's a waste to take in only two. Find a family with four kids who are going to have to buy an extra full-price child's ticket, and offer to take one of their children through with you. By charging the parents half the price of a child's ticket, you subsidise your own entry fee and the other family saves money too.

Blag a tip
When taking children round a museum, give a small talk about the paintings whilst holding aloft a bright umbrella. Pick out clusters of people who could easily be a formal group – but aren't. Speak loudly. Get a friend to present the first tip with a flourish and the rest should follow.

How to exploit adolescents

Let them sulk
Acne and depression come with the territory of being a teenager. If they are reluctant to be seen around, take advantage by never inviting them down from their bedroom for dinner or taking them on holiday. If they complain, say how you thought they 'hated the sight of you'.

To encourage teens to leave, make them get a job and charge rent on their room. If they run away, change the locks.

Oldest swinger in town
If you're acting as a taxi service, but don't fancy being at your teenager's beck and call, benefit from their need to be picked up from evenings out. Turn up early so that you can be part of the in-crowd. And encourage them to have boyfriends and girlfriends over eighteen, then steal them.

It's confiscated
Be brazen and raid their rooms for illicit fags, booze and drugs. You have the perfect excuse for confiscation and you get some payback for all the money the kid has cost you. Why buy your own when your teenager has a ready supply?

blagging it...
mind, body and soul

How to blag more friends

Lost all your friends? Are all the people you know too bland? Here's how to blag your way to greater popularity.

Put people in your debt
Scour your loft to find things that you don't need – and others don't want – as gifts. They'll feel obliged to repay you somehow.

Start a cult or become a prophet
If you can't attract fans with your own natural charm, start a religion or cult. Local directories and the Internet can direct you to plenty of strange organisations. Knock up some prophecies and start holding your own fringe meetings. People will flock to you. They may be sad and vulnerable – but, hey, you haven't got any other friends.

Alternatively, start a wacky protest movement. Take to the streets against something – anything. Make a placard and walk around shouting for free beer or less monitoring of your thoughts through the electricity sockets. The people who talk to you will be either (a) equally mad or sad, or (b) sympathetic souls you can exploit.

Appear unstable
No true friend is going to ditch you if it might push you over the edge. So fake depression when your friendships start to ebb away.

Beware. Crying wolf may put people off. So make the problems real enough. Slight over-dramatisation is preferable to hysterics. No one likes a misery guts.

My old mucker

Join a schoolpals' reunion website and exaggerate your success and wealth. Old acquaintances will come out of the woodwork, determined to re-establish relationships. You may even get your old bully back, but when you haven't any real friends, anyone will do.

How to blag it at dieting

From Dr Atkins to slimming drinks, a whole industry is making millions creating new ways to help us lose weight. But you can fight the flab without shelling out on fad dieting books.

Eat more

It may sound like madness, but if you increase the frequency of your meals your metabolism speeds up, you burn more fat and thus lose weight. Never skip a meal, especially breakfast. Of course, you do have to start eating healthy stuff too.

Make meals last longer, too. If you take at least twenty minutes, your stomach will automatically tell your brain that you are full. The food also goes cold, and unappetising.

Simply add grapefruit

Add grapefruit to your diet. Research reveals that adding the low-cost fruit to meals could help you lose weight – possibly a pound a month – without you having to drop anything else in your diet. Also eat negative-calorie foods – those that use more calories to chew than they contain, like cucumber and celery.

Donate an organ

Why carry extra weight unnecessarily? Sell a kidney and you shed a few grams at the same time. Your appendix and tonsils could come out too.

Water way to go

Diarrhoea causes dehydration, and dehydration causes weightloss. So you benefit, unless you die.

Sweat buckets

Turn up the heating, or spend time in overheated places like department stores. As sweating will make you lose weight, save money by ditching your deodorant too. You must drink lots of water to keep the sweat pouring.

You might consider relaxing in a sauna, where the weight will also drop off (although it takes a long time). To save paying for a proper one, stick yourself in the kitchen, close the doors and windows and bring lots of saucepans to the boil.

Fat congregates

Move to a place with fewer fatties. This will help you feel more guilty about your weight and it's natural to try to fit in. London is the UK's thinnest city, but if you don't fancy a lifetime in the capital, or indeed losing weight, try instead the place with the highest number of fat people. In 2003 that was Glasgow and in 2004 it was Manchester. You won't feel out of place in these cities and are less likely to be called 'Fatty'.

Grub for the grub

A tapeworm can do wonders for your figure. Since the 1920s, overweight people have swallowed worms that act as parasites to devour the food in their stomachs. A rake of celebrities – including porky opera singer Maria Callas who almost halved her body weight – have allegedly used the worms that attach themselves to the intestine of the host. You eat as usual, but lose weight because the worm gets the grub, not you.

How to make easy money from your body

Beautiful body? Someone, somewhere is willing to pay for a bit of it.

Hair today, gone tomorrow
It's free to grow and as you have a never-ending supply (unless you're bald), why not make a mint from your hair? The world's wigmakers will pay £3 to £5 an ounce for good samples.

Sell sperm
You get between £20 and £40 cash in hand for each vial you fill at a UK sperm bank. However, new laws may mean that any resulting children might one day knock on your door – and that could cost you.

As a private transaction, someone may be willing to pay you an awful lot more if you're a stunning looker or dead brainy and they want to have your babies.

Go to work on an egg
It's illegal for women to sell their eggs for profit in the UK, but entirely legitimate in other countries, including the US. So start an export business and earn about £5,000 a time.

Model for art classes
Beauty is in the eye of the beholder – and artists sometimes need to paint or draw ugly people too. You can earn up to £20 an hour by simply sitting still for a few hours.

REAL-LIFE BLAGGER

Piero Manzoni: flushed with success

Wily artist Manzoni canned his own excrement and managed to convince rich people to buy it for the same cost as the market price of gold. Although he made a fortune from his faeces, Piero died before he could benefit from the Tate Gallery's £20,000 purchase of his tinned turds.

How to take advantage of being old

Have more babies

It's the tried-and-tested way of having someone to run round and attend to your every need when you're past your own sell-by date. Beware: you need to work on this before old age sets in (women only).

The more children you have, the more you can exploit their anxiety to get their hands on your money. Make it clear that the one who is nicest to you gets the lot. This will encourage a competitive spirit among siblings – with attendant gifts, company and support for you.

Fake senility

Not everyone who is old is senile, of course. But many younger people treat the elderly as if they are fools. So fool them, by exploiting your age:

- *Free travel:* when caught without your travel pass, get hesitantly to your feet, stuttering: 'How did I get here?' If it looks like you've just wandered away from your home, they are unlikely to fine you.
- *Fake shakes:* help yourself to larger drinks when your shaking hand causes the bottle to tip more into your glass.
- *I've led a good life, your honour:* if you're in trouble for cutting down someone's hedge, confiscating a football, skateboard or Space Hopper (you can get loads of good stuff using the 'confiscation' line), or thumping a neighbour with an annoying beard (which should be justification enough), then the courts will look on you more favourably if you are of advancing years. Everyone may be equal in the eyes of the law, but the closer you are to the grave, the shorter your sentence.

If you do go off the rails at an advanced age, your family may arrange to put you in a home where you meet new friends, enjoy waitress service at mealtimes and have nubile young people to change your clothes and bath you. The added benefit is that you spend your family's inheritance (always a good thing).

How to blag more at the doctor's and in hospital

The compensation culture

Always go to the hospital after an accident, however minor, whether you are hit by a car or trip over a kerb. You could be entitled to compensation and doctors will provide a note describing your injuries.

You want to stay

Most people try to avoid hospital, but if there is a choice between being cared for at home, or being admitted to hospital, get checked in. Unless you're exempt, you normally pay for prescription drugs, but they will pump you with whatever you need for free when you take a hospital bed. You also save on bills at home and get free meals. You can often get more than one free feed by asking catering staff at the end of their rounds if there are any meals left over. There are always people too ill to eat and these days hospital food is pretty good.

Beat the ten-minute rule

Most patients are only allocated ten minutes per appointment, so clock-watch to make sure you get more time than this and you're already beating the system. Of course, someone else in the waiting room may suffer, so lend them this book while they're waiting.

Ask for more expensive drugs

Many surgeries prescribe cheaper drugs to save costs. This means you may not be getting the latest medication because it is usually more expensive. Do a bit of research and then insist on the more expensive treatment. Your GP may relent if you sound as if you know what you are talking about.

Conversely, don't be tricked into paying for a normal prescription for drugs that are cheap. Some antibiotics, including penicillin, cost under £3 on a private prescription. In the normal course of things, these drugs subsidise the more expensive ones. Check with your doctor and ask to go private for the cheap drugs, or buy them over the counter if that's a cheaper option.

Free counselling

Need someone to talk to? Don't pay for a shrink. All they do is sit there and listen – they rarely tell you how to solve your problems. Look for people who don't have any choice but to listen to your woes, like pub landlords, the clergy and deaf people.

How to blow it all before you die

Spend up

Dying rich should not be your life's objective. Living well is preferred. So be a SKIer (Spending Kids' Inheritance). Your aim should be to spend your last penny on the last day.

Someone else will then have to pay for your funeral. If you leave money, these costs will come out of your estate. Don't leave an estate.

On the cards

In your rush to spend every penny before you go to meet your maker, don't forget to blow your credit cards to their limit. Under the Banking Code, your credit-card company will write off the debt, provided your estate doesn't have any assets – and, of course, it shouldn't have, because you've spent the lot.

Milk others from beyond the grave

If you work for a largeish company, you may enjoy a death-in-service payment. Die and get paid up to four times your salary. In fact, many employees would be very rich indeed – if only they were dead.

If you know you're on your way out – and you're unmarried and in an occupational pension scheme – get hitched. Your spouse will benefit from a widow (or widower's) pension.

Pension schemes have caught on to this one and, generally, you need to survive for a certain period after your marriage, usually about six months. But do so and you pass on income for the rest of your spouse's life. Not much good to you, arguably, but it's a useful way for your loved one to milk a pension fund quite legally.

To take advantage yourself, marry someone who is terminally ill but who has a good company pension scheme.

How to get your funeral on the cheap

Even if you spend up before you snuff it, someone has to cough up on your behalf for a funeral. You leave a substantial bill for funeral director's fees, burial plot, smart coffin and fashionable service. If you want to go off in style, on someone else's bill, that's okay. He who calls the funeral director pays. Not you. However, if you do want to save money, tip off your relatives about the following.

The council option

If no one is willing or able to pay the bill, your local council has to stand you a funeral. It may not be a very good one, but hey, you'll be dead.

Also, the government pays a funeral allowance of £600 in extenuating circumstances (under the Public Health – Control of Disease – Act 1984 Part III Disposal of Dead Bodies Section 46, if anyone asks).

Cut out the unnecessaries

Usually, funeral costs include the services of a funeral director, a minister or someone else who conducts a service, flowers, coffin, crematorium or plot, and newspaper announcements.

Do without as many as you can. Not only can you do without a funeral director, remember:

- You don't have to have a ceremony – and even if you want one, you don't have to have it in a crematorium or church.
- You don't have to have a religious minister or anyone else who is paid to say a few words.
- You don't need a hearse: a van or large estate car will suffice – but if you do want a hearse, some funeral directors rent you one separately without you having to pay for a full funeral.
- You don't have to pay for a plot – the fields are cheap, and lakes, mountains and seas plentiful (though easier and cheaper if you're in ashes form for these options).
- If you want to stay close to home, rest in peace in your garden – not usually suitable for flat-owners, admittedly.
- You don't have to have a coffin – but if you decide it's what all well-dressed corpses are wearing, buy one direct from the manufacturer. Many will do next-day delivery, just in case you haven't planned ahead.

Go green when you go stiff

A good send-off can be executed cheaply and with dignity. Use a cardboard coffin. Or a paper shroud (they're actually more expensive than cardboard, as they have to be of sufficient quality to carry a corpse. In fact, a paper coffin could set you back £600 or so if it's professionally made. A bed-sheet is cheaper).

To save yourself about seventy quid, don't hire a vicar – and don't buy an expensive burial plot. Take the environmental option. The Natural Death organisation at *www.naturaldeath.org.uk* can advise.

Burial at sea is one of the cheapest ways and is tremendously environmentally friendly (the fish eat you). A licence, from the government department Defra, is free, but there are only three sites off UK shores.

Not entirely legal, but most environmentally friendly of all: have yourself composted.

Get stuffed

Legally, of course, your body has to be disposed of. If you were an animal, and, in particular, if you had antlers, you could be mounted on the wall. Taxidermy is worth a try. Stuffing a loved one can be cheaper than a funeral and makes an unusual home decoration.

A process called plastination preserves human remains very well and you get to go on the stage if you can sell your remains to a theatrical artist. Surprisingly and sadly, more bodies are on the market than there is demand for them.

In the name of science

Avoid all costs by donating your body to medicine – if they'll have you. There's not much dignity in it, because when they're eventually done, your remains will be thrown in with lots of others before being sent off for disposal. The medical school pays to have you picked up from wherever you're lying – you have to be declared completely and irrevocably dead – and covers the costs of getting rid of what's left over when they're finished.

However, not everyone is accepted. You might get sent back to your loved ones if the medical school doesn't like the look of you. So if you die suddenly, or in an accident, or have donated some of your organs, you won't be wanted.

A gift they'll never forget

The rules on disposal of corpses allows you to surprise someone you don't like.

Tell the medical world that the despised acquaintance is your next of kin. Then donate your organs and ask for the rest of you to be donated to medical science (the offer will be rejected). Your acquaintance will end up with a cadaver clogging their living room – and not disposing of it properly, of course, is a crime. They may not afford you all the trimmings associated with a posh send-off, but there's no coming back from this final insult.

REAL-LIFE BLAGGER

Vuk Peric: gravedigger

This Serbian pensioner faked his own funeral so he could find out who would turn up. He sent out funeral invitations and put a notice of his demise in the local paper, then watched the actual service from a distance. After eventually revealing himself to the assembled mourners, he invited them home for a wake. Afterwards Peric tried to sell his grave and tombstone. Now, having identified true mourners with his fake funeral, he knows exactly who to leave money to when he eventually does bite the dust.

How to get someone to leave you something in their will

Track down long-lost relatives before they die

Genealogy is a thriving hobby, so no one will be surprised if you start digging into your family tree. Search especially for relatives who have no immediate family. The fewer surviving relatives there are, the easier it will be to ingratiate yourself into their affections – and the larger your share of the eventual cake.

Save a life

Nothing is more likely to endear you to someone than saving their life – unless they were attempting suicide. A quick, unexpected shove or shout of 'Boo!' at someone walking along a canal path provides the perfect opportunity for you to become a hero and jump in and save them. You gain a lifelong friend and eternal gratitude.

Choose who you live with

If you have shared a household with someone for two years before they die, you can mount a legal challenge to their will if they haven't left you anything. You have to contest the will within six months of the grant of probate.

How to get a free haircut

Bald readers should proceed to the next section.

Models required

Don't let the word 'model' put you off. You may be dog ugly, but if you've a fine head of reasonably clean hair, there's a trainee hairdresser who's ready – and in some cases obliged by their boss – to give you a trim and even a bit more style.

Seek out one of the trendier establishments. Don't expect an old, grumpy barber to do you any favours when you walk in and declare you're a model come for your free hairdo.

The upmarket chains are on the lookout for a regular flow of new manes.

Save their aching feet by volunteering. Some may charge a nominal fee, but you're still getting a decent cut for a fraction of the price.

Let them draw blood

At the very least, a slightly cut throat will get you a discount.

A sudden, involuntary shudder at an opportune moment when they're faffing around with their scissors can make a cut small enough not to hurt but large enough to draw blood. The more fuss you make, the bigger the discount. Scream a bit and they'll be so keen to shut you up, the haircut could well be free.

A less risky, less painful way is to smuggle in a bit of fake blood (available at all good joke shops or theatrical suppliers) and smudge some on when the hairdresser wanders off to get the hairdryer or fetch you coffee. Tell them they've sliced the head off a mole and it could prove dangerous to your long-term health.

Hasten baldness

Most men fear baldness – but the baldie-look can be fashionable. There will be less hair to look after, fewer trips to barbers and no more jibes about the colour of it (if ginger or grey). Follow these guidelines to help the onset of hair loss:

- Get stressed – a well-known cause of hair loss.
- Go on a crash diet – a proven way to shed excess hair
- Go on the pill. Young women can lose hair with the pill, and as women's haircuts are considerably more expensive than men's, the associated saving is worth much more. Okay, so you probably won't look too great, but baldness is good for the purse and is sure to garner the pity of friends. There's a slight chance you might even look good – think Sigourney Weaver in *Alien³*.

Make a cheap wig

Once you have figured out a way to go bald or have your hair permanently removed, you needn't splash out on expensive wigs. Simply sew your pet's hairs, commonly left around the house, into a cheap toupee. Alternatively, ask a hair salon for some of the redundant human hair that clogs up their floor.

REAL-LIFE BLAGGER

Donald Trump: entreprenhair

Even the rich don't shell out for haircuts. Billionaire building tycoon Donald Trump was plagued for years by rumours that his straggling locks were a wig. However, Trump says that his hair is real and its shaggy, windswept look is because he only allows his girlfriend to cut it. Trump's book *How to Get Rich* even includes a chapter on 'the art of hair'.

How to do your personal hygiene on the cheap

Most people won't really care whether your whites wash whiter, as long as you don't actually smell. But looking and smelling good costs you dear. Here's how to blag personal hygiene.

Hair

- *Shaving:* Sikh men don't cut their hair, so it's worth changing religion if you're not Sikh. Women should consider permanent ways to prevent hair growing, like electrolysis or laser treatment. Befriend a trainee beautician and get them to test their developing skills on you for free. It may be horrendously painful, but you'll have hair-free legs for life.
- *Cleaning:* don't bother washing hair. According to the old wives' tale, it cleans itself after about a month. If you insist on washing, save on shampoo by using washing-up liquid. Use mayonnaise or raw egg to condition dry hair by leaving it on for twenty minutes and then rinsing. Baby powder can also be used as a dry shampoo to absorb greasiness.

Teeth

- *Cleaning:* make a toothbrush by finding a twig and wrapping a strip of velcro around it. One of the flaps on your anorak that you don't know how to use will have spare velcro. Use baking soda to whiten instead of the more expensive toothpaste. In fact, before the advent of toothpaste, people used coal and it worked.

- *Oral hygiene:* instead of splashing out on dental floss, use those little threads that come out of old towels. And chew sage, which you can grow in the garden, to cure bad breath. Have teeth made out of wood instead of expensive dentures – if it was okay for George Washington it's okay for you.

Face and skin

- *Moisturising:* don't buy expensive moisturisers. Olive oil works brilliantly on a washed face – but it is expensive. You will find it cheaper to dip your face into the bowl they bring with your bread in restaurants.
- *Spots:* cover acne by bandaging a large part of your head and telling people you have suffered an injury. This will ensure sympathy instead of laughter or horror. Alternatively, wear a balaclava.

  You can also mix aspirin and water into a paste and apply to blemishes before going to bed rather than spend money on expensive creams.

Armpits

Deodorants are pricey and have been linked to breast cancer. Save cash and your health by switching to remedies found in the kitchen cupboard:

- Apple cider vinegar adjusts the chemical balance of the skin, so that bacteria can't thrive. Bung some in your armpits and say 'So long' to the pong.
- Baking soda is a tried and tested way of killing underarm bacteria and helps absorb perspiration.
- Radishes and turnip juice make great odour beaters. Blend either of them into a mulch, extract the juice, then simply apply to your skin. Keep your fresh deodorant cool by putting leftovers in the fridge for later.
- If you must use deodorant, wait till you get to a friend's house – or posh hotel – so you don't waste your own.

How to blag fitness

Buy the mags
A running magazine on your coffee table or in your bag makes it look as if you take fitness very seriously. Why run when you can read?

Get your heart-rate racing
Aerobic fitness is good for you. You need to get your heartbeat up for twenty minutes or so three or four times a week. Thinking about exercise should be enough to do it.

Timing is everything
Find out when your friends have appointments they can't possibly change, then challenge them to a game of squash. For greater realism, turn up on their doorstep in your kit and with your squash racquet, slightly out of breath, and tell them your playing partner has backed out. They won't be able to join you, but they will be impressed by your commitment.

Use your natural physical assets
Choose a sport that's right for you. If you're fat, try sumo wrestling. Cricket is ideal for those who don't like moving around quickly. Yoga may suit too: blag it by sitting around with your legs crossed.

Get a vibrator
Why bother with sit-ups, when you can strap vibrating pads to your bellies to do the hard work for you? The pads contract and relax the muscles, producing the same effect as exercise and firming your flab into a washboard stomach. Beware: vibrating pads can cost more than £100 a set, but they're the kind of thing people buy and use once, so pick them up from the classified ads.

How to blag beauty

Get yourself a pedigree dog
Show dogs need their hair brushed, split ends fixed, fur fluffed out and claws varnished just as much as preening females of the human variety.

Invest in a photogenic pedigree pooch and get your cosmetics sponsored. What the dog doesn't need, you can use yourself.

Mariska, a borzoi star of the Westminster Kennel Club Dog Show, only uses Canadian hair products, supplied by a sponsor.

Frequent trendy toilets

It's not only the prestigious hotels and nightclubs that provide a bit of scent and sucky sweets. Keep a note of the places that provide freebies and nip in for your fix.

You can even get a decent wash-and-brush-up in burger restaurants like Planet Hollywood, and it's often so busy you can slip through without buying a meal – but stay clear of the times when it's full to overflowing and you have to queue.

Pop into posh hotels

Hotels are not public places, so they can turn you away, but the larger ones are so busy it's easy to slip in if you're reasonably presentable – and don't break the rules.

London's Savoy, on the Strand, in common with many of the finer establishments, has a nice uniformed attendant, who brushes the specks off your clothes as you wash your hands after availing yourself of the bog (they use a different name, but you get the gist). They have top-quality soap, a little perfume or aftershave, and though you're meant to leave a tip, they are far too polite to mention it if you don't.

Men should be aware that they won't get through the Savoy's lounge without a jacket – although they will lend you one if you're otherwise presentable enough. Because the nice man will brush you down, visiting the loo is also a handy way of getting old jackets spruced up without taking them to a dry-cleaner's.

Save on shampoo

Don't believe the bottle. It only says 'rinse, repeat' because the sales director's targets doubled and he wanted to make his bonus. Wash your hair once – and preferably when you're at a mate's house.

blagging it...
at work

How to get paid to do nothing

All pay and no work ...

Get suspended and wallow in paid time-off. This can be tricky. You need to make sure that you do something bad enough to get you suspended from work on full pay, without actually being sacked. Have a friend make an outrageous complaint about you, then get them to withdraw it just as the legal proceedings start.

You could try contradicting your boss in meetings or in front of other workers – something you can put down to a mild difference of opinion, but just enough to be very annoying over a long period of time. They may try to ease you out of your job, with a good pay-off to prevent you taking them to a tribunal.

Gardening leave

Fix yourself up with a new job with a competing firm and your old company will show you the door pronto, but will keep you on the payroll till your leave period is up to avoid you passing on the latest developments to its rival. You won't be able to start your new job, but will be compelled to spend your time having fun on full pay.

Love litigation

When they're tipsy, encourage friends to write nasty things about you, just for fun, in front of other people. Then accuse them of libel.

In the eyes of the law, they have published a defamatory remark about you in front of others.

Blag cash out of your defamed reputation by hanging around courts and getting yourself photographed near criminals. Newspapers that use your picture rather than the criminal's, a not entirely uncommon mistake, could be liable for defaming you.

Also consider changing your name to that of a criminal or one of the people in the firing line of newspaper columnists. People have won cases against newspapers where it wasn't made clear which 'John White', for example, the journalists were slagging off. Naturally, Americans lead the way, suing everyone, everywhere. Sue your parents for genetic disorders and your neighbours when you accidentally slip on their path.

Date criminals

Face it, how often does the gangster's moll go to prison? Living off a bank robber is a risk-free lifestyle – at least, there's little risk from the law. As long as you don't aid their crime or know exactly where their money came from, you probably aren't committing a crime. So date them, live off their loot, then report them to the police (for the reward) and get the authorities to give you a new identity.

Line up some cash

Police are always looking for people to appear on identity parades. All you have to do is to stand in a line in a room with the real suspect and they pay you. And don't worry, they can't arrest you if the witness gets it wrong and picks you. So if you look like a criminal, there's easy money to be made.

You're unemployable

The state will pay you if you can't find a job. Be useless, be unpleasant, be overqualified. And if they do force you to get a job, make sure it's one where you can sit and do virtually nothing, like minding a room in an art gallery or selling skiwear in the height of summer. Why not apply to be a film censor? You're able to watch all the new releases for free and then get to stop other people seeing them.

The drugs are free

Be a guinea pig in drug trials and pharmaceutical companies will pay you to sit around in hospital watching television. You may not even have to be admitted if they don't need to monitor you that strictly – you just turn up for occasional check-ups and have to complete some forms. As they have to test the new drug against a placebo, you might find yourself being paid just to eat sugar pills.

You're a work of art

Throw something together on a canvas or collect some old engine parts and you too can be a modern artist. Take your artwork to a modern gallery and put it on display when the elderly supervisors are dozing – together with a label with your name, phone number and title of your piece.

Then issue a press release and send it with a photo to your local paper. Your crumby artwork gets status, and the value of it soars. If possible, get a friend in a European capital to buy your first piece of work for a nominal amount, so you can truthfully claim 'a collector from London/Paris/Milan' has already bought some of your art.

REAL-LIFE BLAGGER

Dennis Hope: satellite salesman

An entrepreneur who laid claim to the moon in 1980, Dennis Hope has been busy selling it off ever since. Exploiting a loophole in the 1967 United Nations Outer Space Treaty – which forbids states, but not individuals, from owning bits of planets – he has transformed himself from unemployed ventriloquist facing bankruptcy to millionaire – making over £4 million from flogging off lunar land.

There are now satellite operations all over the world. MoonEstates, a Cornwall-based UK franchise, can sell you an acre of the moon for £20.

How to blag qualifications and knowledge

Need to know more about a subject or show off your prestigious educational pedigree? Can't be bothered with all the effort of studying? These ideas will help you look brighter by blagging a bit of nous on the cheap.

Quote Churchill

Never in the field of human communications, has any statesman said so much. When you quote Churchill, no one can ever prove that he hasn't said what you claim, and it always impresses.

Learn while you sleep

Playing tapes to yourself while asleep can plant knowledge without you even trying. Psychologists at Boston University say that the human brain has subliminal learning skills when exposed to a repetitive signal when you're in a light, drowsy state. Hypnotism can also help you remember stuff, so try it before taking crucial exams.

Crib other people's work

It's a fair bet that anything you are ever asked to write or create has already been done by someone, somewhere else. Using the Internet, you can usually find the information you need to crib homework, complete a piece of research for work or justify an argument.

Beware that blending other people's work into your own is technically stealing, but as long as you never copy things word-for-word, you should get away with it. Even the British intelligence services do it – they have been known to incorporate a PhD student's work into the odd dodgy dossier.

Go to an affiliated college

If you can't get into a top university, try one of its affiliated colleges. They often have lower entry requirements, but you get your degree from the more prestigious establishment.

Or just attend another college in the same town. So when you're asked where you went to university, you can honestly say 'Oxford', even if you went to Oxford Brookes University (the old poly).

REAL-LIFE BLAGGER

Jeffrey Archer: lording it up

Take a leaf out of Lord Archer's book. Although he ended up in jail for perjury, he had previously fibbed his way to success. Archer claims to have been a student at Oxford, yet while he never went to Brasenose College, as he stated on his CV, he did get a diploma from the Oxford Department of Education. He convinced people that his credentials were better than they were and eventually became deputy chairman of the Conservative Party.

How to blag your way through an interview

Before you can idle your time away in a job, you first need to land one. Here's how.

Stalk the interviewer

People want to employ others just like themselves. So find out who's likely to interview you and get to know them inside out. Sit in the company foyer and take note of what they are wearing. Drink in pubs near the firm's offices. Discover where they live. Research their biography on the company website, on schools' reunion websites and on Internet search engines. Who knows, you might even get chatting to your prospective employer by accident.

Don't tell the whole truth

Don't give people ammunition to shoot you with. Lying on a CV could get you fired, or even land you in prison. However, leaving certain bad points off your résumé is just plain sensible. It's not illegal to exaggerate. Play around with job titles. If you were a filing clerk call yourself a 'data-storage specialist', and dustbin men are refuse-management operatives.

If you want to get ahead, get a voice

Sadly, some accents are not as desirable as others if you want to get ahead in life. This is regional racism, but it's as well to temper your tones if you have a very heavy accent. In the US applicants with a Southern drawl are most often recommended for lower-paid jobs. Mimic the accent that's sought after by the employers you're trying to impress.

REAL-LIFE BLAGGER

Bob Monkhouse: conniving comedian

The funnyman began his illustrious television career by blagging his way into a job with the BBC. Following National Service, he convinced an RAF psychologist to state that only an audition would cure his 'delusional psychosis'. The doc's note did indeed get him an audition – and the kick-start he needed for a lifetime's work on television.

How to blag your way through work with minimal effort

The art of appearing busy

Got nothing to do? Concerned that someone may dump a pile of work on you? Mask your laziness with frenetic activity. Hurry down corridors clutching files. Make imaginary phone calls. Phone places where you know you will be put on hold for ages. Get angry. How can you not be working if you occasionally swear about how something is going wrong? But mutter your expletives – you don't want to do it so loudly that people come over to help.

Computer error

Load your computer with unnecessary programs that make it run slower. While you're waiting for the PC to process information, sit back and relax. If the boss questions you, just blame the machine.

Think drink

Drink lots – then you can legitimately spend more time in the loo. Few people are ever sacked for comfort breaks. And a drink on your desk is an invitation for it to be knocked over. At the very least, you spend time mopping down your desk, and you may even gain the secondary, but much more valuable, advantage of a saturated keyboard.

Smoke like a chimney

Ever been jealous of how smokers are allowed to go for smoking breaks, while those that don't puff can't pull the same trick? Research by American scientists showed that smokers are less productive partly because they take smoking breaks. Yet bosses – especially bosses who smoke – often tolerate them. So take to the weed if you want to work less. True, you may die earlier, but this means you save cash by not having to bother saving for a pension.

REAL-LIFE BLAGGER

Jayson Blair: story-seller

You couldn't make it up. But he did. This *New York Times* reporter was fired for making up stories and copying other people's work. Among his falsified stories, he claimed to have interviewed the parents of a US prisoner of war in Iraq, even though he had never met them. Once exposed, Blair faced financial ruin – but made up for it by selling his memoirs for a six-figure sum.

How to blag a day off work

Throw a sickie

This is the all-time favourite and not so much a blag as a way of life. It's always more convincing to take more than one day off at a time. Remember to sound the part when phoning in. Party all night before calling so you sound rougher. Then spend your day off in the pub so that, when you appear in the office the next day, you look terrible.

A communicable disease is always a winner. They won't want you around if they think you're infectious.

Malaria is a useful affliction to blame after a trip abroad, especially as it can reoccur for years.

More exotic still, rabies engenders great fear. So foam at the mouth to get yourself a much shorter day. It's an old Stan Laurel trick: tell everyone you were bitten by a dog on the way to work, then, shortly after starting the day's toil, pop an Alka-Seltzer under your tongue and wait for the foam to froth. Rabies is highly contagious and unpleasant and you'll be sent home before you know it.

Act strange

Sickies are suspicious: much better to get sent home by a manager twenty minutes into the working day. True, you will have made the slog into work, but there's always something better to do than toiling.

Feign dizziness, wheeze uncontrollably, generally look peaky and you could be on your way if you have a sympathetic boss. Take advantage of in-house nurses, if you have them, as they always err on the side of caution if you make up symptoms that are too complicated for them to understand.

If the boss is one of those people who is never ill, and frowns on such weakness, better to phone in or …

… hit the fire alarm

The traditional schoolboy blag always comes in useful for an hour out in the fresh air.

Start a duvet-day scheme

Everyone is wise to the way of sickies, so some companies have now caved in and, when someone can't be bothered turning up in the morning, allow a 'duvet day'. There's usually a limit to the number of days you can call the boss and say you're not coming to work, but it's a useful way of legitimising your laziness. Encourage your firm to start such a scheme.

Take advantage of leap years

If you're a monthly-paid employee, every leap year you give your firm an extra day's labour for no pay. Just because there's an extra day in the year doesn't give capitalists the right to exploit you. Take 29 February off – or an adjoining working day if the 29th falls at a weekend.

Get your family to take up different religions

Employers will often agree when you ask for a day off to celebrate a religious festival. Exploit their tolerance by ensuring that each member of your family has a different religion. Choose from major faiths like Hinduism, Islam, Buddhism, Shintoism and Judaism, as well as more obscure sects like Caodaism. Of course, you have to be with your family for important religious holidays. It's hard for a boss not to allow you to attend your son's bar mitzvah, celebrate Diwali with your Hindu spouse or allow you to spend time at work praying, whatever your religion.

How to blag a sick note

Sick notes are valuable. If you earn an average UK salary of £24,500, each day you take off is worth £104. Convince a doctor to sign you off for two weeks and that's more than a grand in your pay packet – just for staying at home!

Look the part at the surgery

Skipping sprightly to your feet when the receptionist calls your name is likely to raise suspicions when you later suggest that working may seriously damage your heath. So:

- Walk slowly.
- Ease yourself into a seat.
- Dress for work: as if you're intending to go straight back to the treadmill after your appointment.

Key claims

A successful sick note blag demands an illness for which no guaranteed treatment exists:

- Stress and a bad back are the only two ailments sufficient to blag yourself a couple of weeks off work safely.
- Express general symptoms, not specific ones. Remember, doctors are professional people, ruthlessly trained to spot a shirker. By being specific, you could inadvertently reveal yourself to be a fraud or, worse, end up having an exploratory operation.

Stress

- Stress manifests itself by headaches towards the back of the skull, sleeplessness, sometimes tearfulness.
- You've been taking aspirin for five consecutive days and are now following the instructions on the label and consulting your doctor.
- If questioned about work, you love it, there's just so much to do, so little time to do it. Get caught working on papers while you wait in reception. Have your mobile phone interrupt your consultation. Don't answer it, just apologise.

Back pain

- It's the commonest incurable complaint. Because it has multiple causes and many people genuinely suffer from it, your doctor will find it hard to dismiss you as a fraud.
- You've noticed that the agony comes on after prolonged periods of sitting (if you have a desk job) or standing (if you don't).
- If you're fat – or preferably obese – a sedentary job exacerbates back pain. Emphasise how confining your job is.
- If you're lean, say how you need to cure this problem so you can get back to your sporting hobbies. Vigorous sports, particularly football or gymnastics, are great for twisting backs.

How to blag a pay rise

Take the credit when work goes well

Second nature to seasoned blaggers. Thank those lower down the ranks for all their hard work on a project, but present it as your own idea to your boss or in large meetings.

The facts of life

If you know you're pregnant, now is the time to ask for a pay rise. Once you get it, your maternity leave will be calculated at the higher rate of pay. Pregnancy is also the time to renegotiate all your loans, your mortgage, and to take on any new financial commitments your expanded family will need, as you won't be able to borrow as much money when you're off work.

Say you'll quit

Bosses don't want to lose good employees; it costs a fortune to find replacements. And it can make you look assertive if you just march right on in there and ask for more money. If you don't want to be so direct, start a rumour that you're leaving. This way you play on your boss's paranoia and when they confront you, simply say that you have no plans to leave, but that a pay rise would make it certain that you'll stay.

Drink with the enemy

See and be seen. Fix a drink date with your competitors in a place where you know you'll be seen by others. When it looks as if you're going to defect, you're in a better bargaining position – unless your boss wants rid of you.

Ask for more than you expect

Ask for an outrageous sum, and try not to laugh when you're doing it. This shows you mean business, and when your boss knocks you down to what you really expected in the first place, you will both feel better.

REAL-LIFE BLAGGER

Maria Popa: professional partner

This Romanian woman managed to convince her downtrodden husband Nicolae to pay her £350 a month – simply to give him a quiet life. The businessman, fed up with his wife giving him grief when he came home from work, struck the deal to stop her moaning. Mrs Popa said she would demand double the salary if they had a child.

How to blag your way to the top

Get one over on your mates

Aim to destroy the reputation of your colleagues whenever there's an opportunity. It's easier if these are your friends, as they will be

·unsuspecting. So go out of your way to be friends with everyone – then it's a breeze to stuff them.

Use your in-tray as an out-tray

As work piles up, swap your in-tray label for 'out' – giving the impression you've slogged your way through a pile of work.

Although beneficial, the danger is that your real out-tray (now marked 'in') suddenly looks bare, causing people to think that you haven't enough to do. Engage in a flurry of paper-based reorganisation, sorting your now thoroughly confused paperwork into what's really in and out. It's easy on the brain and makes you look extremely busy.

Get your boss fired

Everyone makes mistakes; everyone takes the odd thing from the stationery cupboard; everyone slags off their superior. Your boss does all of these. Log his or her violations meticulously and use a tape recorder hidden in your pocket to monitor any transgressions. Then send the whole lot anonymously to your boss's boss.

Alternatively, use your boss's computer to access dodgy websites.

REAL-LIFE BLAGGER

Juan Potomachi: dead lucky

Talk about corpsing on stage – death wasn't going to stop this Argentinian businessman making his way in the world of acting. A hopeless thespian, Juan fulfilled his dreams of treading the boards by leaving a large fund for trainee actors in his will on the understanding that his skull would be used in a production of *Hamlet*.

How to blag it as a boss

Meetings, meetings, meetings

There's always an excuse for skiving off work early or coming in late. You have to interview someone for a job and, so as not to arouse suspicion with their current employers, you have kindly agreed to see them either before or after work, off-site somewhere. Naturally, when the fictitious person you have interviewed turns out not to be right for the job, you have to keep repeating the exercise.

The art of delegation

Managers manage. Underlings do. The beauty of being a boss is that you never really have to work. All the textbooks and training courses teach managers how to delegate tasks to their employees. If you end up doing anything at all during your working hours, you have failed in your duties. When you kid subordinates into thinking you're doing them a favour by trusting them to take on extra responsibilities, they will be grateful that you are supporting them in their careers.

Buzzwords that baffle

All work has its buzzwords and acronyms. Make up a few and use them in conversation. If anyone asks you what they mean, just shake your head, look disappointed in them, then walk away.

You're fired

Sacking people often falls to middle managers, but you don't want to appear to be unpleasant, of course. So be extra-specially nice. Tell your departing underling how you feel their real talents are being held back in their current job. You wouldn't want to be responsible for them not achieving their true potential as that wouldn't be fair. It won't be until security has helped them from the premises with all their possessions in a black bin bag that they will realise they've been fired.

Set hunters on staff

A common way of getting rid of people without doing the dirty work yourself is known as 'head-shunting'. Your firm pays for a headhunter to call your failing employee and flatter them with the offer of a move to another company. That way you don't have to shell out on redundancy and, contrary to the reality, the employee thinks they're too good for you.

REAL-LIFE BLAGGER

Billy Tipton: sex-change saxophonist

In the sexist early years of the twentieth century, Lucille Tipton realised that her dream of making it as a jazz pianist and saxophonist would be hindered by one big hurdle: she was a woman. By pretending to be a man, 'Billy', she landed a job in a band in Kansas City. Over the years, she toured the States with a number of bands, none of which twigged she was female. She even married four times, telling successive wives that she had been in a terrible car accident that had left her hideously disfigured and unable to give them children. Only her parents knew the truth – fellow musicians and the rest of her family only discovered that she was a woman after her death in 1989.

blagging it...
at home and in the car

How to make your house price soar

Add a blue plaque

Blue plaques commemorate a famous former dweller in your property and can do much to push the price of your home higher. The more famous the resident, the higher the demand from fans. With under 1,000 blue plaques in England, mostly in London, Liverpool and Birmingham, there's a scarcity value that could shove your asking price up a couple of grand. Apply to English Heritage if you have a genuine former famous resident – or make your own plaque if you haven't.

Research the history of your home to find an interesting nugget to advertise on a plaque. For new developments, look into the background of the land on which your home is built.

Exhume bodies in the garden

If anyone in your family has followed the advice on page 72 and had themselves buried in the garden, exhume them before your home goes on the market. A grave in the sales particulars can reduce the value of your home by 20 to 50 per cent.

Smell sweetly

Baking fresh bread and brewing coffee is a tired way of covering up for the unpleasant odours in your home. You can do better. Burn a vanilla pod, use aromatherapy oils and bring in fresh flowers.

DDIY (don't do it yourself)
Invite a television makeover team to do up your home ready to sell – then stay. 'It's so lovely, I couldn't possibly leave now,' you can say. Get them to knock down a few walls to create bright open spaces – thus leaving you with fewer surfaces to paint in the future.

How to blag a cleaner home

Give the appearance of cleanliness
A bit of disinfectant at your front entrance will make your place smell fresh. No need to actually clean. The indoor equivalent is to spray polish around your house. Why polish when the smell fools all?

When dusting, only ever do what is at eye-level. Human skin accounts for most household dust. So wear an oilskin to catch the particles.

Animal instincts
Get a dog and keep it hungry. It will lick your plates clean. But at the first sign of fleas or shedding dog hairs, can the canine.

Domestic pets can also sweep the floors if they have long tails. Most neighbourhoods have animals roaming the streets needing good homes. Kittens can be picked up free from owners who suddenly find themselves with half a dozen new feline faces to feed.

If you're happy to have a larger animal around, goats make the perfect lawnmowers, and can provide milk and cheese.

Get rid of older children
Throw out messy children, teenagers, and all pets except the plate-cleaning dog with the long tail. Western children live in a super-sterile world in which they fail to develop immunity, leaving them vulnerable to common bugs as well as asthma and allergies. So it's good to keep them outside. Children who spend a lot of time with animals are far less likely to have allergy problems, so keep them all in a pen in the garden.

Invite an obsessive home

Befriend someone with an obsessive-compulsive disorder based around cleaning, a 'clean freak'. Clean-freakery has become a recognised condition and, as the stigma has reduced, more sufferers are coming out of the closet – leaving it spotless.

Use vinegar for everything

Every household expert recommends vinegar for cleaning just about anything. Never buy an expensive cleaning product again. Just use vinegar, it's cheaper. Put large amounts on your fish and chips – and then you get it free.

De-clutter

Why clean when you can just throw everything away? Start with all the attachments for your vacuum cleaner. No one knows what they're for.

Decorate to disguise

Paint everywhere black – it doesn't show up the dirt. Put down dark carpets or don't have them at all, they show up the dirt more than floorboards.

It's murder

Manage to get on the 'prime suspect' list of a local murder hunt and the police will do a marvellous job vacuuming all the carpets. They may even lift the floorboards and go through your cupboards – and, unless they want to be sued, will put everything back perfectly.

Trick others into cleaning for you

Get a vacuum-cleaner salesman to come round and show off his machines. Some firms that advertise this service promise to clean one room as part of their presentation when they come into your home. Say that the carpets are different in every part of the house and that you want a demonstration in each room. By inviting a salesman each week, you could have effortless cleanliness for months.

Don't worry about it

It's healthy to be dirty. The Japanese, the world's cleanest race, are absolutely obsessed with cleaning. As a result, they could die out within a hundred years, says one of their professors of parasitology.

The UK spends almost as much on household cleaning products as the whole of Eastern Europe. Yet Brits suffer more allergies than their Continental counterparts. Understand that obsessive cleanliness creates drug-resistant superbugs. So stay dirty or die.

How to make money out of your house

Lights, camera, action

Whether you live in a fairly ordinary terraced house or a gothic mansion, a film crew needs you for commercials or drama. You may have to move out for a few days – and you may want to if they're going to do awful things to your home like set it on fire – but they pay well, and they will put everything back as they found it, if not better. You may even get the odd room redecorated.

Ask your regional film commission what kind of properties they need on their books.

If your house looks good in photos, interior-design magazines may be happy to pay to feature it. You don't need to kit it out with expensive furniture. In fact, you could flog photos of a run-down hovel if you throw in a few 'rustic' accessories. Design mags are suckers for this kind of thing.

Take in guided tours

People travel miles to gawp at gardens, so sell tickets for a tour round your own – large or small, wild or cultivated, doesn't matter – and set aside your kitchen as a café area.

In fact, if you don't overprice yourself, you may be astounded by how many people will part with a pound or two to look round your house too. Stick an advertising board outside your front door and buy yourself a little book of raffle tickets to use as entry passes – or, better still, stamp the back of visitors' hands with indelible dye.

For added income, produce a guidebook on your home computer.

Sell off your period features

Many people are unhappy with their brand-new homes. If you have antique cornicing and a feature fireplace, rip them out and flog them.

How to cut the price when you buy a property

Do your own conveyancing

Here's a bit of maths. Solicitors charge about £100 an hour, or thereabouts. Conveyancing – the legal process you go through to buy a house – costs about £350 plus VAT. That means they spend about half a day on your work.

Save money. Get a library book or go on a website and do it yourself. Conveyancing is all about filling in forms and ringing people. HM Land Registry can sell you the forms for less than £15. Visit *www.landreg.gov.uk*.

If you're willing to invest a couple of days' work getting to grips with the forms and the process, you can save hundreds of pounds.

There's a ghost in my house

You shouldn't pay an arm and a leg when there's a torso under the patio. So find out what's been going on in the house you intend to buy – and if there are any skeletons in the seller's cupboards, dig them out before you put an offer in. You can make a killing on a house that's been the scene of a murder, as ghosts really do knock thousands off the value. True, you'll have to live with the ghoul, but you can always have the place exorcised.

Impersonate a builder

Qualified surveyors are members of the Royal Institute of Chartered Surveyors, but there's no reason why you shouldn't disguise yourself as a builder (low-cut jeans, pencil behind the ear, usual phrases like, 'Big job, it'll cost you'). Armed with your own negative report, you can knock the cost of the expected repairs from your offer.

Buy a house no one else wants

Numbers 13 and 666 are considered unlucky, which seriously affects the value of these addresses. Not only can you get more for your money by targeting these homes, but once in you may be able to change the number in order to make it more re-saleable.

How to blag security in your own home

You're a psychopath
The police will happily keep an eye on you if you're likely to kill. The danger is you may be sectioned under the Mental Health Act, but then you get free bed, board and drugs that make you sleepy.

Keep geese, not dogs
Dogs are expensive and want to be loved. Geese, on the other hand, will happily graze all day, get threatening or make a noise if anyone comes close, and require almost no maintenance. Frighteningly aggressive, they have scarily serrated beaks – enough to see off any unsuspecting trespasser.

They also make: (a) very good lawnmowers (b) nifty duvets, and (c) delicious foie gras, which is tremendously expensive in shops and restaurants. It does much to keep the other geese on their webbed toes when one of their number goes under the axe.

Some farmers will give geese away free, but expect to spend about a tenner if you have to pay. If you fancy something exotic and even more violent, get an ostrich.

Put up a false burglar alarm
Easy to do and all the more realistic if you disturb your neighbours by playing the sound of an alarm going off for a couple of hours every Sunday afternoon.

Record a very-large-dog sound
Faced with a house with a dog and a house without, burglars will always choose the easy option. But you don't want the hassle of owning a dog, so blag one. Signs like 'Beware of the dog' or 'Trespassers will be eaten' are tacky, but a recording, perhaps linked to automatic security lights, will do much to keep you safe (if awake) at night.

REAL-LIFE BLAGGER

Robert Merkel: pet-rifying homeowner

Miami resident Robert Merkel never has a problem with burglars, after being granted permission to keep a fully grown tiger in his garden. Neighbours say they are quite happy with Robert's 900 lb pet. One said: 'I get a thrill hearing her roar in the morning.'

How to blag it when buying a car

Choose the right colour

Follow a few simple rules when picking the colour of your new car: it affects the resale value. There's not much of a market for brown cars and green ones are bad luck (so they'll be cheap to buy and hard to sell). Unless it's a sports car, avoid yellow. Ferraris should be red and executive cars blue or black. Metallic paint is best for saloons.

Silver cars are the least likely to be involved in crashes, and black, brown or green the most likely.

Shop at the end of the month

Car dealers usually pay their sales staff by commission at the end of the month. To meet targets, they are more desperate to sell at this time and could give you a better price.

Get the most out of the test drive

Make the most of your test drive, especially if the dealer isn't bothered about coming along. There's no strict time limit, so go shopping, pick up the kids or drive someone to the station.

Go with someone older and wiser

Avoid being taken for a ride by the seller. Go along with an older man, dressed in overalls, who can shake his head wisely and tut-tut, drawing in his breath sharply now and again as he looks over the car.

The trade-in

When a dealer is looking at your car, have brochures from other dealerships lying around on the seat, to appear as if theirs isn't the only marque you are considering.

REAL-LIFE BLAGGER

Edd China: front seat driver

Edd China built his own street-legal motor for just a few hundred pounds, by getting an old leopardskin sofa and creating a car around it. The motorised living room has indicators hidden in two ornamental pots, a pizza pan for a steering wheel, a drinks can for the brake and a coffee table acting as both bumper and dashboard. It even has an in-flight TV and is powered by an engine from a Mini. To prove its road-worthiness, it has an MOT and a road-fund licence. Check it out at *www.cummfybanana.com*.

How to sell your old banger

Round the bend

Your car isn't going to look good parked in an average street next to bins and alongside a load of other average cars. Tell your buyer you live in a more upmarket street and park your car there while they inspect it. They will be more likely to trust you, you should get a better price, and you can play to any upwardly mobile aspirations they might have.

Prepare for the test drive

If your car is temperamental, give it a good run just before showing it off, so that it fires up first time. Make sure the tape deck or CD player comes on automatically with soothing classical tunes. A baby seat in the back suggests you have been a careful driver.

Don't talk about the car too fondly or refer to its pet name – you sound silly and like someone who can easily be knocked down, and preferably over. Remove furry dice and silly stickers saying 'My Other Car's a Rolls-

Royce'. Buyers need to look upon the car as theirs, not yours, from the moment they arrive.

It's in demand
When the buyer turns up, it's ideal if you are just finishing off showing the car to someone else. Have a friend shake your hand and walk away cheerily. People will be more anxious to clinch the deal if they think others are interested in it too.

Choose the right season
In winter, show off your car in the dark and rain – to hide scratches – although convertibles sell better in summer. Avoid the period straight after Christmas when everyone's short of cash. Don't try and sell a car just after the most recent registration plates come out, either. Other 'traded-in' cars are then on the market and they suppress the price.

How to blag cheaper motoring

Become a Sunday driver
There's a reason that all those people idle along the roads. They're not bad drivers – they're just trying to save money. So, any day of the week, annoy other road users by driving slowly. Above about 55 mph most cars become less efficient, costing you more in petrol. Other ways to save petrol include coasting in neutral downhill (dangerous), keeping windows closed (to avoid drag), turning the engine off in stationary traffic and always parking so that you can drive off in first gear – mucking about in reverse uses more fuel.

Lighten the load
Lighter cars use less petrol, leaving you with a heavier wallet. How often do you use those seats in the back? Take them out before setting off anywhere. In fact, gut your car completely. All you really need is your seat, seatbelt and the controls. An extra 48 kg of weight (an average twelve-year-old) can increase your fuel bill by 2 per cent. So keep twelve-year-olds out, or charge them for the journey.

Have music blaring from your car

Turn up the stereo! Because people are more likely to notice you on the road – and be a touch frightened – they are less likely to bash into your motor.

They will also think you are some kind of gangster, and that if they don't let you through first they might get shot or have their vehicle rammed. For the same reasons, you should also drive a car with a vivid colour. This is good because slowing down and changing down gears isn't fuel-efficient.

Go surfing

Just like racing drivers, you can use another car's slipstream and so save petrol. Drive close behind big lorries (not *too* close) and you benefit from the wake they create, lowering the wind resistance on your own car.

Find a car-friendly environment

- Live somewhere flat so that you use less petrol.
- Live somewhere warm. Colder engines use more fuel because a higher percentage of fuel condenses on the engine parts.
- Move to Iraq or any other country where you don't have to have a licence (but watch out for bombs and bullets which might damage the paintwork).

Stop your car being stolen

- Put a dent in it yourself, or cover a bit with cardboard to make it look as if it is in need of repair.
- Buy an ugly car.
- Keep it dirty.

Save money on expensive personalised number plates

Change your name to match the number you already have (this blag was suggested by R760 DGF of London).

Blagging it when you park

You're a doctor on call

If there's a medical emergency, it would take a hard-hearted traffic warden to give a doctor a ticket when he or she was saving lives. But, of course, it's criminal to pretend to be a GP, so get a PhD. There's a bit of study involved, but there's bound to be some tinpot university that will award you a doctorate for the minimum effort. Once you're officially a doctor, you can leave a 'Doctor on Call' sign in your car with a (relatively) clear conscience.

Removing the iron boot

You'll need a Stanley knife or equivalent. Jack up the affected wheel, cut through the tyre sidewall at the back and pull the tread inside out. Then remove the clamp, fit your spare wheel and leave the clamp undamaged. The replacement tyre will cost you less than the clamper's fine, given that it can be as much as £250.

If you take the clamp away, it's theft, so do leave it for its owners to pick up. And do remember, if you've parked on a double-yellow line, or in another area monitored by council traffic wardens, you're breaking by-laws and will have to pay a fine anyway – unless you can charm the traffic warden, which is unlikely. Once they've started writing the ticket, it is notoriously difficult to cancel.

If you damage the wheel clamp, you may find yourself busted for criminal damage. You should only be so bold if you are absolutely certain you've been clamped illegally by an unscrupulous firm. If this is the case, it's possible to use bolt-cutters on the locks of many clamps – and you may consider suing the company for any damage to your car, such as chipped paintwork.

Clamp yourself

It isn't illegal to clamp your own car. So, if you're parking somewhere dodgy, use your own clamp. You can buy them cheaply online and they have two benefits. While busybodies and wardens will imagine that you have already been dealt with, a clamped car also fends off potential car thieves.

Clamping is an unlicensed industry, so for a bit of fun you could even set up your own firm and clamp real nuisance motorists. Why not start with those urban, road-clogging 4X4s parked outside schools?

REAL-LIFE BLAGGER

Angle-grinder Man: wheel-clamp wizard

Kent-based superhero Angle-grinder Man helped countless hapless motorists escape from wheel clamps – after he was clamped himself in a hospital car park after being told to park there by a supervisor. Wheel-clamping firms didn't complain about having their property sawn off and, with no crime reported, the police couldn't do much about it.

How to get ahead in traffic

Drive a hearse

It's remarkable how many drivers refuse to overtake hearses. So drive one and you will always be at the front of the queue. You get the benefit of holding everyone else up.

You can find one in the 'classic cars' section of magazines like *Autotrader*, or simply enter 'hearses for sale' into a search engine on the Internet. With an understandably small market, they are surprisingly plentiful and joyfully cheap.

Antiquity helps

If people think you're old, they will let you out at junctions (unless they're young, in which case if they think you're old, they cut you up. Sadly, you have to be able to spot the age of other road users with this blag).

Drivers of shiny new cars are also much more cautious about drivers in old motors. They have much more to lose in the event of a bump. A knackered old 4x4 with a tow-bar can do much to help you muscle your way into parking spaces ahead of everyone else.

Your passenger is having ...

... a baby, if female.

... a heart attack, if male.

So you need a police escort.

Use taxis

It's usually cheaper to use taxis than it is to run a car. The average cost of running a car in the UK is more than £3,000 a year – so you could spend £60 a week on cabs and do away with the stress of motoring.

How to blag a test drive in an obscenely expensive motor

Swanning around in a posh motor is a joy in itself, and, as you will impress other people, it's also a passport to other luxuries, a beautiful date, or an invitation to more parties. A blag to get a blag, in other words. Try these tips:

Phone ahead

Salespeople at the top dealerships can smell a timewaster before you even get through the door. Preparation is everything.

A call before your visit will pave the way. You are ringing to discuss your requirements. Explain you're in the market for A, but are considering B, and have already tried C, which you liked, but the waiting list is too long. Before wasting either your time or the salesperson's, you want to check the finer points.

A car magazine, or the columns of the weekend papers, can guide you to the right questions to ask.

Turn up in an expensive motor

If you blag a test drive without the salesperson accompanying you, you could go from one dealership to the next and impress every one with your current set of wheels.

If not, and you don't know anyone who can lend you such a car, it's wise to park round the corner rather than turn up in a 1984 Ford Escort.

Get on the right list

It's astonishingly simple to get invited to drive away in a gleaming machine worth tens of thousands of pounds. Log on to the manufacturer's website and request a brochure and you have started a relationship the dealer will want to build upon.

There's usually a box to tick saying you would like a test drive. You will soon start to get invited to model launches and open days – and as a car is usually a very occasional purchase for most people, they won't be too surprised when you don't write out a cheque there and then.

If all else fails ...

... get one of the prestigious car badges from a scrapyard and stick it on the car you drive now.

How to get out of paying a speeding ticket

Speeding, of course, is an offence, and can have very serious consequences. You may be lucky just to get away with a ticket, but money, licence points and your future insurance premiums are at risk. If the ticket is incorrectly completed in any way, appeal.

- Check your ticket. Police officers do make mistakes (Guildford Four, Birmingham Six, now you). So if it doesn't have the right date – which occurs particularly at the beginning of the month or year, when the rozzers have to meet their targets – contest it. You can probably prove you were somewhere else.
- Has your number plate been entered correctly? A slight slip here and you could claim they nabbed the wrong car.
- Don't sign the chitty, as it's tantamount to agreeing to the crime.
- Radar doesn't give accurate measurements for approaching cars, so if they've taken you from the front, it's worth appealing.
- If you've been caught by an officer brandishing a mobile speed detector, challenge its roadworthiness and ask for it to be verified. It has to be calibrated pretty ruthlessly, and if it isn't up to scratch, you're off the hook.
- Try to get the police officer not to write the ticket in the first place. Ask for a warning. Elderly gentlemen, grannies and attractive young women have most chance. Be polite and don't argue. If you have a bad attitude, you've got no chance of getting off.

It wasn't me, guv

If you've been caught by automated equipment, blame your passenger for the offence, while they should do the same and say it was you. If the police don't know who was at the wheel, you stand a good chance of getting off because of a legal loophole. But beware, you may be committing perjury, and that could mean jail – but, hey, what's a bit of time with paid bed and board when the alternative is money and points on your licence?

This blag works particularly well if there are several named drivers on your insurance policy, or you have given permission to lots of friends to drive your car whenever they want to. If you have a company car that every member of the entire workforce might possibly drive, all the better.

Remember, you can't deliberately obstruct the police, but if you say you have thoroughly investigated and can't find the culprit, what else can you do? Just because you're the registered keeper of the car, you weren't necessarily the one behind the wheel.

REAL-LIFE BLAGGER

Christine Hamilton: amnesiac traveller

Cheeky Christine Hamilton avoided a speeding fine when her car was clocked at 63 mph in a 50 limit through motorway roadworks. She told a court she had 'no idea' whether she or her husband, former MP Neil, had been driving – so the courts didn't know who to nick. The judge said he had 'no reason to disbelieve her'. Mrs Hamilton declared it a 'victory for motorists'.

---

blagging it...
in entertainment

How to blag a free drink

Scamming a free drink is easy when you know how.

Ask for a sample
You wouldn't buy a car without taking it for a test drive, so when you want to get your body well-oiled ask to try the drinks first. Most bars will let you test the beer before buying. Try four or five, say they're not to your taste, then move on to the next place. It works with wine as well as beer.

'You spilt my drink'
Towards the end of your drink, bump into someone, making sure you spill your dregs over yourself. They're sure to buy you a new drink, especially if you get a stain on your clothes.

Make sure you choose the right bumpee. Pick the geek or wimp, not the beefy rugger-player or madman who is going to start a fight. Men should never bump women. You'll end up having to pay your own dry-cleaning bill, and possibly hers too.

Act depressed
Walk into a quiet pub you don't know, sit down at the bar, put your head in your hands and wait for the barman to ask what's wrong. Tell him you've been made redundant, your partner's left you and your dog has just died. Compensatory drinks from the barman and the locals should be forthcoming.

When it's time for your round, fake a call from your boss or partner in which they appear to have changed their mind and want to see you straight away.

Be a professional beer taster

Top brewers frequently need beer tasters to help them make sure their product is tip-top and to test new lines. You can even take courses in it. 'Sensory evaluation of beer for microbrewers' is a popular weekend booze-up in the US, taught by esteemed professors. If you drink a lot, why not start your own course?

Alternatively, the government funds wacky university research projects of all kinds. Apply for a grant that allows you to study, say, the persistent use of alcohol in people who don't like to pay for anything.

Take the piss

Take an empty beer bottle into the toilets and fill it with urine. Back at the bar, complain that your beer isn't cold. To save time a puzzled barman will simply give you a fresh one.

If he takes a sip, agree with him that the beer tastes like piss.

Take communion

It's only a sip, to be sure, but needs must when the bottle is your friend. Check out times of services and, if they're staggered in your area, you could teeter round to several churches and end up with about half a glass of red inside you before lunch.

How to get served first at a crowded bar

Use these wily ways to outwit other jostling boozers and get your drinks first.

Learn the barman's name

Get to know the barman or barwoman's name either from someone else in the pub or by asking when you buy your first round of drinks. More simply, read their name badge. Then, rather than queue with the hordes, simply shout out, 'Another pint of lager please, John!' (or whatever is relevant). They will think that they know you and, even if they don't, once eye contact has been made they should feel obliged to serve you.

Wave your cash

The best chance of speedy service is to look earnest and eager. Holding up a crisp note in the air also helps, but don't wave it around too much – it simply looks pushy.

Only tap coins on the bar if you want to wait around half the evening.

Blocking strategies

Lean forward and make yourself big. Stand with legs apart and elbows out. This will help block other people trying to get to the bar, without you having to resort to shoving. Never make eye contact with anyone else at the bar (except John the barman), and definitely don't strike up a conversation. Your body language should say that drink is your priority, not niceties. If you are out with someone else, you should both queue up and simply hand over the cash to whomever gets served first.

Don't become Mr Inbetween

If a number of staff are on duty, they often work different areas behind the bar, dividing their territory between right and left.The middle of the bar is therefore a grey area and you're more likely to be forgotten about. Avoid it.

Stand out from the crowd

Wear noticeable clothes or a T-shirt with a striking message. Alternatively, simply stand behind very attractive or tall people who already have the advantage that they will probably be served quickly, and slide in sharpish the moment they start to move away.

How to blag a free cup of tea or coffee

They are the world's most popular pick-me-ups, but don't spend a fortune buying them at shops and cafés. Here are some easy ways to grab a quick free cuppa.

Seek out accidents

A cup of sweet tea is a well-known cure for shock victims. So hang around hospitals, pretending you have just witnessed a terrible accident – or have one yourself: fall off your bike in a park or simply faint in a crowded place. Someone is bound to bring you a cup of tea.

You're a tramp

Many people will spare the price of a cup of tea. So grow a beard (women should carry a fake one), don dishevelled clothes, and then approach people brandishing an empty plastic cup.

Give blood

You got your blood for free. Donating some of it costs you nothing. You usually get a free cup of tea and biscuits when you hand over your armful. Donate every day. Once the queasiness wears off, you'll feel extremely weak but deservedly good about yourself. If you faint, you'll probably get another cup of tea.

Holy (boiled) water

These days churches often serve tea and coffee after morning service. You don't have to sit through the sermon – just slip in at the end.

Go to church coffee mornings, but steer clear of the ones that are raising money for good causes – they will want your cash. However, if they think they can get their hands on your soul, the church will stump up a cuppa – and possibly home-made cake and biscuits too.

When approached in the street by people wanting to convert you, look as if you're pleased to see them (this will come as a shock). You're interested in their religion, of course, and would like to discuss it over a cup of tea, you should say. Then let them take you to one of the expensive high-street coffee bars, where you can select the largest, most expensive drink and a muffin and listen to their pitch, knowing that their treat has cost close to a fiver.

Visit neighbours

Look for 'sold' signs outside houses and pop in to introduce yourself to the new occupants. No need to live near by, or to tell them where, because they may expect to be invited back. 'I live down the road' is sufficient to quell all suspicions – and on goes the kettle.

There is such a thing as a free lunch

Cut corners when dining …

Be a wine buff

Make sure that you're the one to choose the wine. Scan the list carefully, mumbling about good years and rainfall, thus giving the impression you know what you're talking about. Then pick the second cheapest. You haven't chosen the House Plonk and you haven't blown the bank. So you don't look cheap. The waiter will know what you're up to: Mr One-Up-From-The-House.

If you really can't bear paying more than is necessary for the House Plonk, bear in mind that it is sometimes a better wine that the One-Up-From-The-House anyway. As many people go for the One-Up bottle, crafty restaurants buy cheapest and sell it for a higher price than the House. Inform your partner of this charade and you can choose the cheapest wine safely.

Another bottle please

When you're asked to taste the wine, don't hesitate to send it back if you don't like it. This is etiquette – you don't want to serve your fellow diners bad wine, and why else would the restaurant ask you to try it in the first place? Deciding whether wine is off is pretty subjective. Even if it's a £100 bottle – which, of course, it isn't, unless someone else is picking up the tab – the restaurateur has to take it back and bring you something else.

Don't feel guilty – real blaggers never do. The restaurant will return the offending bottle to their supplier.

Do send back the wine within the first half of the bottle, otherwise you stretch your credibility. However, you can send the bottle back repeatedly, until they start getting shirty.

Take a moral stance

Eat half your food then call over a waiter, look horrified and enquire: 'Were these beans grown in Zimbabwe?' Or, 'These carrots taste as if they were genetically modified.' Count on the fact that they won't know. Immoral morsals don't pass your lips, you should say, making it worse that you've eaten much of the meal. As you would be prepared to sue, another dish should be forthcoming.

'Waiter, there's a fly in my soup!'

Actually, putting a fly in your soup that wasn't there already is fraud – but being fussy isn't illegal. If your food isn't up to scratch, you may be able to leave without paying. So complain about the food if it's not good enough (and learn how to contest the bill – see page 116).

Every day's a birthday

Many restaurants will offer a free cake if it's your birthday or another special occasion such as an anniversary. Some offer free drinks or even the whole meal to diners they know well. So make sure they are informed of the occasion in advance and choose a restaurant where you are a familiar face.

Go undercover

Big restaurant chains employ mystery shoppers to pose as customers who test quality of service. Sign up and you could get paid to eat free meals – and more. In the UK more than 150,000 mystery shoppers enjoy luxury hotels and free cinema visits as well as restaurant meals. Agencies like The Mystery Shopping Recruitment Club operate in the UK, USA and Canada. Recruits, who usually have to write a short report on their experience, can fit visits around other work.

Market munchies

If you know which markets to check out, you can make a meal of your visit. Farmers' markets have some of the finest fresh food in the country, and stallholders will be delighted to let you sample their fare. Of course, they like you to buy something, but it's not compulsory, so you can dine out on top grub for nothing.

Ask at all your nearby supermarkets when the next taste-test promotions are taking place and eat and drink as much as possible at them. The person providing them won't care – they're probably not being paid enough to worry about it, and it's their job to give away all their samples. The company that has hired them will be delighted that their product is so popular.

Break a leg

One of the major benefits of a hospital stay is a uniformed angel delivering a hot meal right to your bed. Worth a small sprain any day of the week.

You also get free meals in prison – which is where you'll be if you follow some of the advice in this book.

Run it over

Next time you're motoring, don't worry about hitting the odd animal. The most edible roadkill are pheasants, partridges, pigeons, rabbits and hares. Go anywhere rural, preferably wooded, and especially near country estates where there are organised game shoots, and the back roads will be lined with dead birds. Pheasants are particularly stupid and their road sense has as yet failed to develop at anywhere near the pace of modern cars.

REAL-LIFE BLAGGER

Alan Conway: Stanley Kubrick imposter

Retired travel agent Alan Conway managed to convince people he was film legend Stanley Kubrick, taking in politicians, theatre critics and even a Hollywood producer. Even though Conway looked nothing like the reclusive director of *2001: A Space Odyssey*, it didn't matter, because few people knew what Kubrick looked like. Entertainer Joe Longthorne allegedly laid on a Rolls-Royce and paid for a luxury hotel for the blagger. Conway also got free entry into exclusive bars like London's Groucho Club, and his new friends in the movie business were happy to pay for all his food and drink.

How to get a better deal in a restaurant

Reaching the end of a meal knowing you have no means to pay then offering to do the washing-up is a crime. Contesting the bill, on the other hand, is fair game.

We've all had meals that aren't all that's been promised. When the food is poor and the service is worse, it adds insult to injury to be presented with a bill. Complain during the meal and they'll add rodent droppings to your next course. Never take another mouthful after complaining. Instead, refuse to pay at the end.

Because taking a meal in a restaurant constitutes a contract agreed only between you and the restaurateur, quibbling about the terms of the contract moves the matter out of criminal law and into the realms of civil dispute.

Negotiating a new, lighter bill

- Make an offer to pay a reasonable amount towards the ingredients of the meal. About a quarter of the price of the food should do – perhaps slightly more in posh places.
- Unless you've sent the wine back, pay for all your drinks.
- Possibly add a small amount to cover anything you have enjoyed.
- Should it come to court, your opponent will argue you have had some benefit out of your visit. Put them on weaker ground before it gets that far.
- Leave your name and address – don't lie, otherwise you move back into the crime arena.
- Don't pay the service charge.
- You pay VAT on restaurant meals, but it's not always listed separately on your bill. Recalculate it on the basis of your much-reduced bill.

If they threaten to call the police, agree politely that their food, service and prices are criminal. Your dispute is a civil matter. The police should only agree. If the restaurant chooses to take it further, it must sue you for the difference between the bill and the amount you have paid.

If you're really blagging, you may wish to settle before it comes to court. Otherwise you'll have to pay their costs too, if they win. However, the bad publicity should put off many restaurants from taking matters that far.

Get friends to pay for more of your meal

When out with friends, you have to establish the ground rules before you order. If it's one of those occasions where you pay for the items you order, pick cheap.

However if you're dividing the bill by the number of diners, this is the most cost-effective way for you to enjoy the very best the restaurant has to offer without paying top whack. It's in your interests to choose the most expensive bits from the menu. Don't miss a single course – and select the finest wine. When you have the most expensive meal, someone else always subsidises you, guaranteed.

Be a critic

You don't have to go to the effort of being recruited by a local rag to get improved service and freebies by posing as a food critic. Rather than telling staff that you're a critic, drop heavy hints that it's worth pleasing you. They know that real critics rarely reveal themselves.

Use these pointers to help word get round that someone important is in:

- Keep an open notebook on the table, breaking off to scribble squiggles that look like shorthand whenever a waiter arrives at your table.
- Dress smartly and keep looking at your watch.
- Have a phone conversation that sounds like you could be talking to an editor.
- Open a well-known restaurant guide to reveal pages covered with annotations.

Pass yourself off as a food inspector

- Purposely get caught sticking a small thermometer into your food.
- Run your hand along potentially dusty surfaces. For added paranoia, wear a white glove for this.
- Fill in forms as the staff talk to you.
- Ask to see the bins at the back of the restaurant.

How to blag your way into a club

Get on the guest list

Send one of your friends to hang by the door and listen for two or three names given by people on the guest list. With the names in hand, chill for an hour at a nearby bar, then head back to the club. After a while these lists become confused and you should be able to get in by proffering a previously used name.

You may also discover that the doormen will read the names out loud as they go down the list, trying to locate someone. Those people may not have arrived yet – but you know who they are and can now borrow their identity for the evening.

You work for the chain

If the club you want to go to is part of a national chain, call ahead a few days before and say you work for them in a different city. Say you're in town and you'd like to check out how they do things at their end.

Not only should your name be added to the guest list, you may even get VIP treatment when you arrive.

Learn the lingo

Top clubs frequently use a password system for guests. In the US, whisper 'Filet mignon' into the ear of a bouncer – it's a well-known codeword.

Use humour. If you make the bouncer laugh they're much more likely to let you in. A phrase like 'I'm a plastic surgeon and I'm needed in there right away' could get you far.

Confuse the bouncer

Let's face it, they aren't always the brightest of people or they wouldn't be standing in the cold while everyone has fun inside. So ...

- If you're under-aged, when the bouncer asks how old you are, tell him your date of birth. He might just let you in, rather than do the arithmetic.
- Get younger people to come along and stand in front of you – you'll look older by comparison.
- Wait for a fight and sneak in while they're preoccupied.

Bounce yourself

If you can't beat them, join them. Learn all the tricks of the trade by going on a course for budding bouncers. The British Institute of Innkeeping's course includes topics such as refusing entry and social skills. Students receive a National Certificate for Door Supervisors.

Be in the middle of an argument

Ignore the bouncer and walk in while arguing loudly on the phone. No one likes to get involved in someone else's domestic.

How to blag your way into a gig

You're making a behind-the-scenes documentary

Find out the name of the promoter and tell them you're producing a documentary which is being 'looked at' by a TV channel. A huge camera isn't necessary as many documentaries are shot on tiny digi-cameras. You can look the part by hiring a camera for under a tenner.

You will get privileged access into secure VIP areas and the chance to interview the stars. You can later sell the tape to a broadcaster – and if not, it makes a unique home video.

Be a hack

Tell the organiser that you are writing a review for a magazine about the city or town the gig is in. Better if it's foreign. As all press passes look different, forge one. Then, when you arrive, lavish praise on the place, saying that the tourist board have recommended it. It's a useful way not only to get into a venue once, but to get invited back in the future.

Be with the band

Carry some gear like a lamp or instrument and you can walk brazenly past security who will assume you're part of the team. Make sure you dress down like a roadie, or up like a promoter.

You're the DJ

Similar to the 'I'm in the band' ploy, with this variation, you walk past security with a box of records or CDs. Beware of using real ones in case they are nicked. A black box with silver buckles can be passed off as the real thing and can be stored in the cloakroom till chucking-out time.

Get the stamp of authority

Many clubs use wristbands to allow customers to go in and out. Keep a wristband collection in different colours to use at the appropriate venue. You may also want to invest in an ink stamp – it doesn't have to be the real thing: once rubbed, it will pass for a pass.

How to gatecrash posh parties

Every film premier, state dinner or VIP bash attracts a batch of undesirable, uninvited guests, many of whom are genuine fans, some of whom may well be mad. You're not part of this unprofessional crowd of gawpers, so you have to perform a better blag to get you through the door. Once you're in, no one wants to cause a scene by throwing you out too violently.

Dress appropriately

A sober suit or dress can be used whatever the dress code – with the exception of the very poshest of black-tie bashes, but you can generally check this in advance. If it turns out to be fancy dress when you arrive, claim you're James Bond.

Formal parties

You can blag your way into formal events at hotels quite easily, by making up a name card from an organisation, preferably foreign, and wandering in. Fake a speech impediment if conversation is above your level. No one is going to ask someone with a disability to leave.

It's surprising how many formal functions will actually hand-write a name badge for you when, good heavens, your imaginary friend has forgotten to call ahead and alert the organisers to your attendance.

Learn to read upside down

This essential skill should be part of every blagger's repertoire. Spot a name – preferably one that matches your gender – and say that it's you. Clearly, if you're five foot two and eighteen stone you can't claim to be Hugh Grant, especially if you're a woman. So you need to scan that list fast.

Don't worry about the real owner of the name turning up later. That's their problem.

Take a bodyguard

Any large, imposing friend will do. Dress them in a black T-shirt, black overcoat and dark sunglasses, and stick a wire in their ear.

A protective escort may be enough in itself to give you the impression of importance, but if problems arise on the door, get your bodyguard to say: 'Mr A [insert your name, don't say A] *is* on the list, sir' in a deep, firm, slightly threatening manner.

Remember, posh parties have their own teams of large, imposing people in black with wires in their ears. You need the biggest.

Look out for launches

Attend the opening bashes at new bars or clubs. Call the day before saying you want to send a letter to the owner. Use their name to get in on the night. Scan seating plans and discarded invitations to learn the names of other guests.

A party of your own

If the bash you want to get into is taking place in a hotel or other location that has more than one function room, ask to check the room out for a large party that you're planning yourself. They will usually turn you down politely, because an event is already going on in the room, but by insisting you only want to snatch a look, they should escort you there. Smile at the doorman on the way in – and on the way out say, 'See you shortly.' Then shake off your escort, go back and walk brazenly back in.

Arrive in a limo

Useful if you're part of a blagging syndicate and can share the cost. Limos can be surprisingly cheap – some illegally tout for business late at night in major cities. It might be worth striking a deal with the driver and have him drop you ostentatiously outside a top nightspot. Or perhaps you could borrow a limo for a test drive (see 'How to blag a test drive in an obscenely expensive motor', on page 106).

Turn up in a laundry van

Strictly speaking, you don't need to bundle yourself into a box with the laundry to get in the back, but do think about where goods are delivered to the venue – you can be sure it's not through the front door. Check out the tradesman's entrance; it's often easier to blag your way through the back than it is at the front.

If the party is being held on an upper floor, consider using the stairs (particularly any specifically for tradespeople) rather than the lifts. Many party venues in big cities are above other shops or offices, so you can visit the ground floor, then leg it up the stairs to the party. Alternatively, go to the venue early in the day, before security arrive, and hide in the toilets.

REAL-LIFE BLAGGER

Aaron Barschak: royal party prankster

Dressed as Osama bin Laden in drag, the self-styled 'comedy terrorist' blagged his way into Prince William's twenty-first-birthday party. Evading the best security Scotland Yard could offer, Barschak climbed a tree, jumped a wall and then strode brazenly into the bash at Windsor Castle.

Once inside, police officers were fooled into thinking he was a genuine guest, as any man sporting a pubic wig and pink frock would be at a royal party. Barschak got as far as the stage and planted a smacker on William's cheek. He wasn't prosecuted for the stunt, got a five-figure sum for his story and went on to relate the tale at the Edinburgh Festival.

How to gatecrash any old party

Time your entrance
You're most likely to be rumbled when the party is at its quietest at the start of the event and the host is able to spend most time with guests. Arrive when everyone is half cut and either doesn't notice you or is past caring, particularly if you arrive posing as a strippagram or a clown with a few magic tricks up your sleeve.

Be a friend
There's a private party going on and you want to go. Think of a common name like Dave or Sarah. Turn up at the door and say you're a friend of theirs. If it's a fair-sized party they'll let you in rather than try and find them.

Target fancy-dress parties
Who's to know you're not invited when you're in disguise? If you do get to meet the host, they will be embarrassed that they don't recognise you.

How to blag your way through a dinner party

Wine tricks
It's good manners to present your host with a bottle of wine in return for your dinner. Naturally, you want to look as if you've bought the best, without having to pay for it. So reuse the bottles that they gave you when they came round to your house (having drunk the wine yourself, of course). Refill the bottles with cheap stuff of your own. (This only works with screwtop wine bottles.) Your friends will note that you've chosen a wine they like (after all, it's the one they gave you), but that, on this occasion, it must be off.

You should hope that: a) they are too polite to mention it, and b) they haven't read this book – otherwise what you thought was a good wine that they gave you was really cheap stuff of their own, in a case of the blagger blagged.

Of course, you don't want to spoil a nice meal with cheap plonk. Suggest your friend 'lays down' the wine for a day or two to let it settle. Using phrases like 'lay down' also suggests you know something about wine.

Dinner at your house

It's good manners to invite your hosts to your house for a return match. This is nearly always an exhausting or costly mistake. Limit the damage by inviting a friend who just loves cooking to arrive a few hours before the start. No need to tell them they will be the first by several hours. When they arrive, say it was an honest mistake, but you're sure you can use the time well. Hand over an apron and put them to work.

Serve ready meals up as your own

Don't go to the length of cooking a three-course dinner. Spice up supermarket ready-made meals by making them look as if you prepared them yourself. You don't have to buy expensive varieties, but do make them look better by employing tricks from top restaurants:

- Serve food on large, white plates.
- Make the portions slightly too small and stack the food in layers.
- Use candles so that your guests can't see their food properly.
- Provide lots of bread before serving the starter so that they won't complain about the small portions later on.
- Add a few fresh herbs and a lemon wedge, sprinkle on some freshly-ground salt and pepper, and drizzle on olive oil to give an authentic home-made appearance.

REAL-LIFE BLAGGER

Antony Worrall Thompson: shrewd chef

A celebrity chef who thought on his feet when asked for a dish he didn't have. The TV cook served tinned tomato soup, tarted up with croutons and basil, to his restaurant customers because there wasn't time to create his own, despite it being on the menu. Fortunately the diners loved it and congratulated him on his creation.

It's not for long

The latest you can ask guests to arrive without appearing rude is 8.45 pm. Hold your dinner parties on Sundays, so that everyone has to leave early to be in a fit state to go to work the next day. Best of all, they will decline your kind invitation to stay longer – so then they feel guilty as well.

How to throw a party on the cheap

Entertaining is expensive. Cut the cost and still have fun.

Cancel halfway through

Ask guests to bring a bottle (champagne is preferred). Halfway through the party fall ill, apologise profusely, and politely ask everyone to leave. They'll be too embarrassed not to leave their drinks behind and you can live it up in front of the TV with the booty.

Punch drunk

Don't buy lots of different expensive drinks – make a punch instead. Buy cheap but very alcoholic drink, like sherry, put it in a bucket, then throw in all the old vegetables and bits of fruit you have lying about. Add a dash of Tabasco or chilli powder and spend the evening boasting about your famous mixture and its 'secret ingredients' handed down by a great-uncle. As long as it gets your guests drunk quickly and there is enough to go round, they won't demand pricey refreshments like wine or whisky.

This shouldn't stop you insisting on guests bringing a bottle in the traditional fashion. Anyone who brings cider but expects wine should be shown the door.

'Of course there's room'

Don't be left with the cleaning to do the morning after the night before. Invite your guests to stay, even though you may not have room or even a spare bed. Let them slump inebriated in the corner when it's too late for them to get a train or drive home. You guarantee yourself a ready-made cleaning corps, available to put the house back together when they wake up.

Your place, not mine

Parties are hazardous, so much better to have drinks spilt and cigarette burns on your neighbour's carpet, not yours. Offer to draw someone else's curtains and keep an eye on their place when they're on holiday – then invite two hundred people round to party.

REAL-LIFE BLAGGER

Miosav Static: the wedding stinger

Serbian Miosav Static became addicted to going to weddings and gatecrashed 1,500 of them. Hooked on the atmosphere and happiness, he said that he was guaranteed a good, free meal among friends (just not his). He cribbed details of the nuptials from local newspaper announcements and always took the bride a gift.

How to blag it at drugs

Here's how to have fun – and get high – with your friends, completely legitimately

Use oregano instead of marijuana

After a couple of beers mix up a joint for your friends using simple kitchen herbs. Oregano looks the part. Watch as you offer them a smoke and the placebo effect takes hold.

Drug alternatives

Plenty of substances that are available over the Internet will give you a high and are not banned by the state. For a bigger buzz than tea, coffee or booze, you could try the herb salvia, a member of the mint family. For an LSD kind of high, take morning glory, also known as Hawaiian baby woodrose seeds. Even eating raw magic mushrooms isn't illegal in the UK, though you risk being poisoned, of course.

You can also give yourself a high by boosting certain hormones in your body. According to scientists, this can be done by eating chocolate or exercising, but experts have also identified that you get the same effect by having a good gossip about other people. This has the added benefit of saving you from having to diet or put in any physical effort.

It's a gas

If your partner if giving birth or your kid is having a tooth out, take a quick blast of the gas when medical eyes are averted. You'll get as high as a kite, gratis. Best not to collapse in giggles when your loved one is screaming in agony, but as pain is relative and relatives are pains, sharing the gas is the least they can do for you.

How to blag it at gambling

Blag it to boost the booty when taking a punt.

How to avoid sharing your Lottery win

Most people who have won the Lottery say that the money has made them happier. So be happy – by following these proven ways of bagging a bigger win.

Numbers to avoid

Stay away from seven – people often pick it as their lucky number. Don't pick numbers that are all in one section of the ticket or ones that are in a row. Avoid commonly selected sequences like 1,2,3,4,5,6. You have the same chance of winning, but you'll be sharing the prize with ten thousand other winners. Don't pick numbers in a symmetrical pattern on the ticket either, as it's extraordinarily common.

Numbers to target

Numbers on the edge of the lottery ticket are chosen least often – and the number 46 least of all. Favour higher numbers because many people link their choices to birthdays, most commonly between 1 and 31.

Other tips:
- Always tick the box requesting 'no publicity'. You can then sell your story.
- Beware: while you may have more chance of winning by joining a syndicate, you bag a bigger, life-changing sum if you play on your own.
- Never buy tickets for more than one draw in advance. If you win the jackpot, you will have wasted £1 on a ticket you don't need.

Don't be a fruit on slot machines

Find out when the jackpot was last won. A rough guide is to leave a machine for ten days between jackpots. Slot machines near the door in casinos pay out more frequently than others, because the owners figure that people will see the coins fall on this machine and will be tempted over the threshold.

Fruit machines are heavily loaded against you. Punters rarely win against machines: best to go for the weakest link in a nest of gambling vipers – other people.

Statistically speaking

To win at games like poker, it pays to be able to calculate the odds of any particular hand coming up. This may not guarantee a win, but it will give you the edge over your rivals. In the end, all gambling is about probability. Swot up your maths and you pocket more cash.

Statistical theory will help you do better on the football pools. Use the Poisson distribution system. Fishy though it may sound, Poisson distribution calculates the probability of a certain number of goals being scored in a match. Find out the goal averages of the two competing teams and you can use it to work out the statistical chances of a specific score.

Goals	0	1	2	3	4 or more
Av. 0.8	45%	36%	14%	4%	1%
Av. 1.2	30%	36%	22%	9%	3%
Av. 1.6	20%	32%	26%	14%	8%
Av. 2.0	14%	27%	27%	18%	14%

For example, if you calculate that Manchester United averages 1.6 goals per match and Chelsea bags 1.2 goals, then you can use the table above to work out the likelihood of certain results.

For instance, for a predicted 0–0 draw, multiply 20% and 30% (0.2 x 0.3 = 0.06) – which is a 6 per cent chance of that scoreline. For a 2–1 United win, multiply 26 per cent by 36 per cent to reach a probability of just over 9 per cent.

If your computer has an Excel spreadsheet program, it has a Poisson function built in and can help you work out these odds. Probably.

Bet the house on bingo

To give yourself the best chance of landing a million quid, play bingo. National bingo games give you eight times the chance you would have of winning the same amount of cash on *Who Wants To Be A Millionaire* (and you can always get a seat at bingo). Boffins say it's also a better bet than sports gambling, the pools or the Lottery.

REAL-LIFE BLAGGER

John Haigh: maths-termind

Maths expert John Haigh has worked out how to increase the chances of winning on top TV quiz shows:
***Millionaire*: if you don't know the answers to the fastest-finger round, the most likely sequence to come up is DACB.**
***Weakest Link*: contestants should bank at £200, if two out of three questions are being answered correctly. Bank at £600 if three out of four are right, and if eight or nine out of ten are correct, then don't bank until £1,000. And if you can work all that out, enter *Mastermind*.**

How to blag it at sport

Being a sporting hero – or even just getting into prestigious VIP enclosures – is within your grasp. Follow these tips.

The winning streak
If you want to be cheered on by a crowd of thousands, but lack any

discernible sporting talent, pull it off by streaking. You'll need a seat near the front and a pair of trainers (the only stitch any decent streaker wears). Traditionally, a helpful policeman lends you his headwear while escorting you off the pitch.

Dying to see a match?

No need to miss a game just because you're dead. Get close to your team by having your ashes scattered on hallowed turf. Many leading football clubs don't allow this in the centre of the field though, because it affects playing quality, but will happily scatter you between the goalposts. You may even get a free ceremony hosted by the club vicar.

When you were in your prime ...

If your sporting days are behind you, or your prowess was never up to much, you can still relive the glory days that never were. Buy trophies for your mantelpiece at car-boot sales and second-hand shops. Athletics impresses more than darts and snooker.

Choose obscure sports

If you don't know who holds the world championship crown for toe-wrestling – which does exist – it may as well be you. An authentic title demands years of practice and dedication, so you may want to create your own championship and be the only contender.

REAL-LIFE BLAGGER

Karl Power: good sport

A serial prankster who first made his name by joining Manchester United for a team photo by dressing up in their club's kit and tagging on to the end of the line-up. Among his other sporting blags, he played a knock-up on centre court at Wimbledon before a match by waltzing past security guards. On another occasion, he appropriated a helmet and overalls to emulate a racing driver so that he could climb the podium after a Grand Prix.

How to blag fame

If you'd like to be famous, blag it to stardom.

The celebrity that no one recognises
Say you appeared in a reality show, or declare yourself the winner of an obscure beauty contest. There is already Miss World, Miss Galaxy and Miss Universe, for example, so turn up as Mr or Miss Milky Way (Mrs Milky Way if you're old).

Behave like a star
Change your name to something distinctive (see page 54). Hand your signed photo to people and send it to autograph dealers. Ask people which celebrity you most resemble and become a lookalike. You don't even need to be pretty: Saddam Hussein used to have lots of body doubles – though, sadly for him, none of them was the one they pulled out of the hole.

Lookalikes earn huge sums and are employed by top footballers and movie stars to divert attention. You will need to keep up to date with their latest haircuts (footballers) and surgery (Michael Jackson).

Once you start being invited on to the party circuit, you can reveal your own talents to the people who matter.

Seek publicity
It's easy to get in the tabloids if you know how. Simply pulling a wacky stunt can land you in the prime spot in the *Sun*. Newspapers are always looking for eccentric characters to make their readers laugh. Why not say that you live on a diet of baked beans and be photographed in a bath of them? Or theme your home, like the man who put a fake shark through his roof.

Box clever get on TV
Apply for every reality and quiz show going. Behave as oddly and outrageously as possible at the auditions. TV executives are looking for the most sparky characters over good looks. They particularly want people who have a low embarrassment threshold.

Exploit any unusual relationships or unnatural fetishes by tipping off researchers on lifestyle programmes. They're always looking for something out of the ordinary.

Become an expert

Journalists and TV talk shows need experts to pad their airtime and qualify their stories. Set yourself up as one by running a course in something unusual, or write a book on something obscure that will interest publishers and hacks alike. *Weeds in a Changing World* and *Guide to Eskimo Rolling* are both real titles that someone had the foresight to publish.

REAL-LIFE BLAGGER

Mark Roberts: lucky streak

Guinness Book of World Records streaker Mark Roberts scored a try during his first streak, at a Hong Kong rugby match in front of 65,000 supporters. Later sponsored by a sportswear company – who presumably wanted him to keep his kit on – and a suncream firm, Mark famously hopped starkers across a weather map of the UK – live on national television. He claims to be a professional streaker and travels the globe baring all before him.

How to take advantage of competitions and promotions

Millions of pounds' worth of goods are given away each year in competitions and promotions. Learn the short cuts that could bring you goodies for free.

Lie on consumer questionnaires

Always say you purchase supermarket 'own-brand' products (or non-branded goods) on questionnaires. It increases the number of free offers of your favourite branded products – those that you are in fact already buying.

However, when completing coupons in newspapers, never say you read the paper every day, thus identifying yourself as a loyal reader who is happy to pay. Instead, tick the box that says you buy just once a week – on the day that the coupon appeared. You should then qualify for discount vouchers.

Stand out from the crowd

Enter competitions using bright postcards and the biggest envelopes to make your entry stand out.

Enter as often as possible, using different people's names and addresses. Make sure they wouldn't mind you using their name first, of course (you don't want them to take the prize should you win). Although many competitions don't allow multiple entries, the reality is that most of them receive so many, it's impossible for them to check.

Use puns when writing slogans for competitions. They can be a key to winning.

Embrace junk mail

Get on mailing lists. Shredded junk mail makes great protection for fragile objects in parcels, or bedding for pets.

Even just going through it can divert you from more arduous tasks at home or at work.

'Free prize draws' in which the winner is pre-determined really do have to give you the prize if you reply and your number has already come up. The downside is that the odds are long. However, you end up with more junk mail. Which gives you many more opportunities to enter. If you keep replying, you will achieve something akin to perpetual motion, plus you could be a winner.

and finally...

How to blag your way out of trouble with the law

Be prepared
If, by some travesty of justice, you are wrongly arrested after reading this book:

You're a Freemason
Lots of judges and policemen are Freemasons, so it may help to get you better treatment from the legal professions. Joining their ranks certainly couldn't hurt. Do it now and start practising your secret handshakes.

Grass someone up
You will need to know some criminals. If you already do, or you're one yourself, you're one step ahead. Informing on people often leads to more lenient treatment – and a brand-new identity in a safe house as a bonus. So start compiling dossiers on your friends, family and acquaintances. You never know when your insider knowledge could get you off a charge.

Lose your marbles
Insanity is a genuine defence in law – and it can be temporary. Arguing

that you were ill or mad at the time you committed your blag could get you a reduced sentence or a long stay in a secure hospital.

In the dock

Once in court, you and your solicitor should work every ploy you both know to get the magistrates or jury to look favourably upon you. Here are some tips:

- Cry – not for yourself, but for your victims.
- Dress attractively, but soberly, in clothes that won't make you sweat (and thus look guilty).
- Don't wear black – the uniform of burglars and gangsters.
- Don't wear loud colours either – the uniform of street rappers, robbers and gangsters.
- If you're under eighteen, your school uniform will make you look both innocent and vulnerable.
- Don't speak unless you are spoken to. Magistrates and judges like deference.
- Don't have change jangling in your pockets. It's intensely irritating – and it looks as if you can afford a big fine.
- Plead not guilty and hope the prosecution service will lose the papers. It happens all too frequently.
- Be pregnant or have young children that you have to look after. This requires a certain amount of forward planning.

our thanks

INSTINCT TOLD US that everyone wants to get something for nothing. Little did we realise how many people, usually upstanding citizens of the highest integrity, practise the scurrilous art of blagging so brazenly.

So thank you to Jim Addison, David Bartlett, Mark Bowness, Carol Dovener, Richard Cullen, Mark Dancel, Adam Goodyer, Peter Halliday, Janette Hazledine, Tamsin Hebditch, Rick Hebditch, Mark Henshall, Toby Holt, Simon Horne, Phil Huggins, Owen Jones, Shawnee Lister, Renata Caruso Lorenzo, Lana Matile, Richard Medley, Geoff Moore, Philippa Moore, Tom Moore, Sam Moore, David O'Riordan, Ruth Phillips, Will Poole, Hannah Reynolds, Sarah Sarkhel, Alexandra St Marc, Daniel Simister, Nan Stuart, Samm Taylor, Paul Waddington, Tony Welford and Seng Yeo – and especially to Nicola Adamson whose uncharacteristic ruse whilst shopping for engagement rings (see page 48) ignited the spark that led to this book. Nicola is now Mrs Ainger, and our thanks also go to husband Robert, who gained a few free glasses of champagne (and a wonderful wife) but lost a small fortune to diamonds.

The idea was the easy bit. Convincing Michael O'Mara Books of the merits of publication demanded one big blag of its own, and this fell to our agent Robert Smith. Robert guffawed over some pages, said, 'You can't say that!' about others, and provided one or two scams of his own in an entertaining page-by-page assessment of an early draft.

Finally we'd like to thank Lindsay Davies, Chris Maynard, Gina Rozner and Sonia Pugh at our publishers, Michael O'Mara. However, since this is a book about blagging we intend to take all the credit for the hard work, good advice and enthusiasm that they have contributed.

Paul Nero and James Moore   *London, July 2004*